ARE THORESEN wa

A doctor of veterinary .... anthroposophic medicine, homeopathy, acupuncture, osteopathy and agriculture. Since 1981 he has run a private holistic practice in Sandefjord, Norway, for the healing of small animals and horses, as well as people. He has lectured widely, specializing in veterinary acupuncture, and has published dozens of scholarly articles. In 1984 he started to treat cancer patients, both human and animals, and this work has been the focus of much of his recent research. He is the author of *Demons and Healing* (2018), *Experiences from the Threshold and Beyond* (2019), *Spiritual Translocation* (2020, all Temple Lodge), *The Lucifer Deception* (Clairview 2020) and several other books on complementary medicine published in various languages.

TRANSFORMING DEMONS

THE TRUE STORY OF HOW A SEEKER RESOLVES HIS KARMA

From Ancient Atlantis to the Present-day

Are Simeon Thoresen

CLAIRVIEW

Dedicated to All Who Seek to Heal and Understand

Clairview Books Ltd.
Russet, Sandy Lane,
West Hoathly,
W. Sussex RH19 4QQ

www.clairviewbooks.com

Published by Clairview Books 2021

© Are Simeon Thoresen, DVM 2021

First published in three separate volumes under the title *The Forgotten Mysteries of Atlantis: In times of the destruction, Re-found in present day Ireland through Anthroposophy, Their Karmic importance for today, Parts I, II & III* on the CreateSpace publishing platform in 2015, 2017 and 2019

First published in this new, re-edited format by Clairview Books

A CIP catalogue record for this book is available from the British Library

ISBN 978 1 912992 26 3

Cover by Morgan Creative
Typeset by Symbiosys Technologies, Vishakapatnam, India
Printed and bound by 4Edge Ltd, Essex

The Angel

The doors are closed.

In one of the doors there is a little window,
and the handle is low enough
to be reached by the one that is small.

The door is open and the new spring air flows in.

Not far away is the cherry-tree filled with its smell
and flowers as white as the full, white moon.

I am newly washed and it is Saturday.

Close to the cherry-tree trunk
a being is standing in the moonlight.

And even if it is day,
and all the others are having their afternoon nap,
the entity is glowing in the dark.

Are Thoresen
1964 (aged 12)

Contents

PART I

Introduction to Part I

This book is about the long path that my friend 'the Seeker' made during several years of his life. This path brought him to the point of confronting his misuse of women, female-energy and power in both this and in many of his past lives. The confrontation with his demons and the threefold confrontation of his karma, referred to in Parts I, II and III of this book, relate to the meeting of his demons in the soul (astral) world, the life (elemental/etheric) world and finally in the body (physical/material) world.

To be able to face such demons in both the astral, the elemental and the physical world, my friend the Seeker had to cross the threshold to the spiritual world in order to enter it more deeply. Such a crossing, and also what is faced and met 'behind' the threshold, is described thoroughly in several of my earlier books,* and I will not repeat it here.

The memories brought to consciousness in this book are found in the flickering of the evening camp-fire of childhood, where the glowing embers awoke memories of old times, and in the glimmering of the ocean waves of youth, where the gentle strokes of the ocean awoke memories of an ancient past.

---

*Especially *Experiences from the Threshold and Beyond* (Temple Lodge Publishing, 2019).

Chapter 1

The Leprechauns (Gnomes) show the Hidden Way. Fire and Cosmic Consciousness

Between 1993 and 2011, after being imprisoned by the dark forces of A. for 10 years, L. intervened and set the Seeker free. He was then liberated from a deep and long-lasting imprisonment by these forces to work further on his karma and the destiny that involved many people.

But let's start at the beginning... In 1992, following an inspiration, my friend the Seeker had travelled to Ireland. He hired a car at Dublin airport and drove to Galway, on the west coast of Ireland. The journey had to start in this area, that once was a part of the sunken continent of Atlantis – a region where the old Gaelic language is still spoken today.

On his return journey from Galway, travelling back to Dublin, he stopped his car at the junction of Ballinasloe. A doubt had entered his mind, a feeling of something important. He wondered where to go, which way to travel? He sensed a call, important to both himself and others. Should he choose the shorter way to Dublin through Athlone, or the longer northern route through Langford?

He stopped his car in a desolate place surrounded by turf and flatlands. As he stepped out to consider which route to choose, the gentle wind took hold of his hair and caressed his skin, as if the country itself, the whole place, welcomed him. The rain had ceased and the air felt pleasant. The smell of the water-soaked turf felt rejuvenating.

He stood there at the junction, completely alone. Then something unusual happened. A movement to the left in the periphery of his vision caught his attention, and he turned his head slightly towards this movement. Two entities were coming towards him. It seemed as if two men were approaching, although he knew it was not actually so. He looked somewhat amazed at the two 'men', apparently human creatures. They were not ordinary men, although they had a human shape. They were what the Seeker later discovered to be pure-bred leprechauns, native to Ireland, that in Norway are called *gnomer* or *nisser*.

They wore clothes that were common some hundred years ago. They had solid boots and green trousers. Their jackets had upturned sleeves and on their heads they wore hats with feathers sticking up, as can still be seen today in Tyrol, Austria.

The leprechauns stopped a few metres away and looked directly at the Seeker. Then, without a word, they both lifted their right arms simultaneously and pointed vigorously and with strong intent in a south-westerly direction, opposite to the north where he was considering travelling. Luckily, he knew that in the 'other realm' – the 'etheric and elemental realm' of reality, in which clearly the leprechauns existed – all things are reversed (as if seen in a mirror), which indicated that the creatures were actually pointing north-east.

Then, suddenly, they were gone, and there he stood, alone once more. However, he was now sure that he should take the northern route, understanding that it was of great importance to travel in this direction.

The Seeker had known the people that lived in the 'other realm' for years. In his home country they were well known, and the Norwegians knew that there were many different kinds of such beings. There were *nisser, dverger, troll, huldre, nøkken, draugen, gråinger, alver, gnomer, sylfer*… and within each group there were many variations.

He had once written a poem in praise of these beings. In this poem he had called them:

The Under-earthlings (The Subterraneans)
A faint breathing in marsh and bogs,
the sun has set.
They are approaching, in their silver-grey lustre,
my world is at peace.
I feel the old parts of my soul
changing and bending in mind,
but this must be my path,
if eternity shall be mine.
I get up in uncertain calm,
they dance their dance.
They spin around, in the sacred ring
being pulled by their own movements.
I'm sinking down in the moonshine,
I know they have to leave,
before the dawn with its sun-penetrating force
breaks their peace.

This was not the first time that creatures from the elemental realm had showed themselves to him. He noticed that the more important it was that he received and understood the messages they were supposed to give, the more physical the elemental entities appeared. This time they were almost totally physical. It was as if they were made of flesh and bone.

The Seeker remembered the time when the huge *draugen** had appeared in front of him, as if it was material, with water dripping down and seaweed between its massive fingers. At the time, he had not known that he was actually in great danger, and later he understood that this creature had saved his life.

He had, at that time, a 23-foot wooden boat with a two-stroke gasoline engine. It was late autumn and he had taken a day off from work in order to sail the boat to its winter resting place. The route he was taking was quite hazardous, past a rocky area of the Norwegian coast where many sailors had drowned and many a small boat had been taken by the waves. This area, Yxney, was also an old initiation place for Nordic shaman connected with the *Drotten* Mysteries, hundreds of years ago. A labyrinth, called a Troy castle, had been made there as part of the old *Drotten* initiation ceremony.

What is a Troy castle?

More than 6,000 years ago, there was a great and catastrophic drought in the area north of the Caspian Sea. This period lasted for 2,000 years and led to the people living there wandering to the west and north-west. Without the use of horses, this movement would have been impossible. On horse-back, these people changed European history forever. They came to Europe in three great waves – each separated by a few hundred years – and, 5,000 years ago, these people influenced the greater parts of Europe and South Scandinavia. 4,000 years ago, the British islands and Iberia (Spain/Portugal) became part of their sphere.

Everywhere that these people came to dominate, the old gods representing fertility and female qualities (the Moon-cults) were exchanged with a war hero on horseback (Odin, the Sun-cults).

The so-called Troy castles are an indication that Asian tradition and thinking was known in Europe long ago. Close to my home in the Norwegian coastal town of Sandefjord is a marine peninsula called Østerøya ('Eastern Island'). About 1,000 years ago, this

---

*Kraken in English. In Scandinavian folklore the Kraken is a legendary sea creature of gigantic size.

land was separated from the mainland. It was an actual island, with a narrow strait used by the Vikings as they sailed between the two main cities of Norway at that time (Kaupanger and Tøns-berg). On the southern part of the peninsula there is an area called Yxney. A part of Yxney forms a separate and smaller peninsula, as an appendix to the main peninsula, the Truber headland (Tru-berodden). Two small fjords, south and north Truberfjord, form this headland. Between these small fjords there is a isthmus – a narrow strip of land, bordered on both sides by water, connecting two larger bodies of land, over which one can walk out to the head-land of Truber. Up to the year 1,800, a strange man-made stone formation was visible on this isthmus. It was a row of stones placed in a special pattern to form a labyrinth. This labyrinth has given the name to the area; as such constructions are called labyrinths of Troy, in this particular case, Truber.

Several labyrinths like the one near Sandefjord are known in Europe, but especially in Scandinavia. From ancient times, these constructions have been called Labyrinths of Troy. Variations of this name, such as Trøyenborg, Trøborg, Trelleborg, Troytown, are found all over Europe. The origin of the name lies in the mighty old city of Troy. Why this name is connected with the labyrinths is uncertain but we may see some relationships if we investigate the ancient city culture of Troy.

Homer's Iliad describes in detail the fierce war between Sparta and Troy. At that time, Troy was the most western outpost of Eastern philosophy and thinking, while Sparta was more western-orientated. The people of Troy had captured and imprisoned Helen, the beautiful princess of Sparta. After several years of fighting, Helen's followers set her free. They managed to conquer Troy with the help of a giant hollow wooden horse, in the belly of which they managed to get into the city. Via the wooden horse, the Western way of thinking gained access to Eastern philosophy. As we will see later, the constructors of the Troy castles possibly were oriental horse-warriors that rode from the east during the time of population migrations and settled in different parts of Europe, especially Scandinavia.

With regard to the Troy castles, there are usually myths about horses, showing that the parallel to The Iliad may be of some value, or at least of some interest. Much that has been written over the years about the Troy castles often mentions visions or myths

A Troy labyrinth found in Finnmark, Northern Norway

of black horses in connection with the labyrinths. In Sandefjord, seamen tell stories about seeing a couple of black horses just before bad weather or storms. Such visions usually encourage the seamen to return to shore. This also happened to me once. If I had not returned at that moment, my boat would undoubtedly have been wrecked in the oncoming storm. A glowing castle has also been observed several times at the headland.

Most of the labyrinths have several other stories associated with them. These stories include the ability to warn of storms, or that a ritual held in the labyrinth would prevent wreckage and guarantee a good catch of fish, as the fishermen would have more power over the winds and the movements of the seawater, as well as over the fish.

Many scientists are also convinced (Colin Bord, Lorens Berg) that there were rites connected to the labyrinths, rites to prepare seamen to cope with bad weather or fish catches, or for horsemen to manage and tame horses. The same scientists have also agreed on the age of these labyrinths and dated them to 1,500-500 BC. It is highly possible that the builders of these labyrinths were Asian shaman, who came together with Mongolian conquerors on horseback during or before the times of the folk migrations.

'Hand of Draugen' by Karl Erik Harr

So, our friend 'the Seeker' was sailing past this old Troy castle. He had to go this way, out into the open sea, passing the rocky area with the Troy castle, and then into a quieter fjord (Sandefjordsfjorden) where the boat was to rest during the winter. As he sailed the boat out to sea, the wind became stronger and stronger. The boat was lifted up by the swell of the peaking waves, and crashed down in the troughs. The engine worked hard, and the small boat rocked in the rough sea. The weather became more and more hostile, almost stormy, but he continued on. After a while he reached the area of Truber, and just before he was to enter the most dangerous part of the journey, something totally unexpected and unbelievable happened. A huge hand, exactly as shown in the picture opposite, appeared out of the sea, coming up from the depths. Water ran down the fingers and seaweed was hanging from the nails… It was a totally natural-looking, physical/material hand, apart from the fact that it was about 8-10 metres high! No arm was to be seen, no body, no head or face – just this enormous hand. Then slowly the hand started to beckon to him, as if it wanted the Seeker to follow down into the depths of the ocean. He was well acquainted with old Scandinavian folklore and immediately understood that it was the 'hand of Draugen' calling him to his death, to drown. In a flash he instantly realized his predicament and made a quick decision – a decision made without hesitation or fear. He turned the boat and sailed with the wind back to the summer anchor spot. As he travelled with the waves and the wind, this part of the journey took only a short time, perhaps 15 minutes.

A few days later, when the weather was calm and still, he tried once again to sail the boat to its intended winter resting place. After just 10 minutes the engine stopped. There was no more fuel! He had totally forgotten to check the level of the gas. If he had continued on his route that stormy day, the fuel would have run out exactly at the most dangerous part of the route. The boat would surely have been destroyed, splintered on the rocks and sunk. He would have been lucky to survive. The hand of Draugen had indeed saved him.

Many years later while travelling on the Hurtigruten coastal boat going from Bergen to the northern border of Russia – a voyage that takes seven days each way – he found a picture based on old Norwegian traditions, showing exactly the same situation. This must have been known from ancient times.

*

Back in Ireland, standing at the junction, the Seeker knew from previous experience that seeing leprechauns in such physical reality brought him an important message, a life-changing message. He was totally convinced that he had to travel via the northern route. He had to travel that way. He sensed that it was vital.

Getting into the car, he started the engine and thus went off in a north-easterly direction towards Longford. The landscape in this area was typically Irish, with green rolling hills, clusters of trees, stone houses, abandoned farmsteads and the occasional modern house dotted about. Cows were grazing, the sky was blue and all was quiet.

After about 90 minutes of driving, just before he came to Longford, he spotted burning grass on the left side of the road, about 200 metres away. The flames were high and fierce and it seemed that the fire was out of control. He stopped the car at a small passing-point on the right side of the road, rolled down the window and looked out.

Again, something unexpected happened. The flames shot up in the air, changed direction and came directly towards the car. They entered through the open window and made a spiralling movement around him, encircling his head and upper body. He was not burned, nor did he feel any discomfort – he only felt a strange sensation of being invaded by something.

He was immediately transported to another realm of existence. For how long was he gone? Where was he? It was impossible to answer, but this experience was of deep and significant importance and full of meaning. It initiated a development which was to continue for years, influencing the fate of many.

What was this experience? He was thrown into a state of complete and total communication with the entire cosmos, on all levels. His *thoughts* were crystal clear, understanding everything. His *feelings* were totally transparent, encompassing all and every single thing in a love so deep and warm that he never thought was possible. His *will* felt as if it could reach the highest mountain top and overcome the most difficult task.

He *was* the entire cosmos. He was one with God.

Eventually he came out of this experience and slipped back into the ordinary world. Exhilarated and dazed at the totality of such a cosmic occurrence, the ordinary world felt so dull, so grey, so disappointing and so depressing in contrast.

One special and interesting feature about this experience – and actually all the other so-called 'supernatural' or spiritual experiences described in this book – is that they are impossible to remember exactly. My friend the Seeker put it this way:

> When I think back on all these experiences, all I remember is the impression I had after the experience was over – after it had ended. I never remember the actual experience

in detail. I do have a recollection of some of the pictures, of the insights, but the details have vanished, as if in a dream. This fact leaves me with an uncertainty, a feeling that it did not really happen; that it was only a memory of something else. However, when I focus on the situation and re-live the experience, feeling the huge impression it left upon my soul, I have never doubted that what I experienced was real. This 'forgetting' of all details of what happens when one is in the spiritual world can also be a problem in my work as a healer and veterinarian. I always make a pulse diagnosis of my patients, and immediately after doing this I forget the results. Sometimes this forgetfulness makes the animal-owners irritated, but there is nothing I can do about it. You see, the pulse-diagnosis is done whilst the therapist is actually in the spiritual world, due to the dividing of his thinking, feeling and will. Experiences in the spiritual are not remembered as are experiences in the physical world.

For several weeks the Seeker felt depressed. Deep depression often emerges after such spiritual experiences, because the memory of them quickly fades away. As they disappear, they leave only emptiness and a longing for what was. Also, spiritual experiences never repeat themselves; they just fade into the bosom of the spiritual world.

*

Some months later, in the late autumn, when our friend the Seeker was safely back in his homeland of Norway, the telephone rang. A man from Stockholm was calling and, without much small talk or explanation, told him the following: 'I represent a group of Swedes that are in telepathic contact with a group of old Atlanteans that are not currently in incarnation.'

The expression 'old Atlanteans that are not currently in incarnation' refers to individual souls of people who lived at the time of old Atlantis, who are at present not incarnated in living, physical earthly bodies like you and I. Of course, most of us have lived in the time of old Atlantis, but have moved on and experienced many incarnations since then. Some souls that lived in old Atlantis, however, have *not* incarnated since the time of the Great Flood, mainly because of their bad karma due to the use of black magic.

The message to the Seeker from the so-called 'old Atlanteans' was as follows:

> We have been told [by even higher spirits, I guess] to tell you that you worked in old Atlantis, as the leader of a group of people connected to a pyramid. This pyramid was situated in the eastern part of Atlantis, in present-day Ireland. You were working there as an oracle,* and as this oracle you had the ability to have absolute and total contact with the entire cosmos.

The man from Stockholm did not say much more. He just stated this and hung up. Why did these 'old Atlanteans' bring forth this message to our friend the Seeker?

There is one obvious explanation – an explanation that our friend the Seeker only came to realize some 20 years later; that the heavy karma of these 'old Atlanteans', his old friends and co-workers of the pyramid, was mainly due to actions they and he had conducted in their work as priests within the Atlantean pyramid. Many of the priests that had committed great sins in those times had not dared to reincarnate. Our friend the Seeker had dared to do this, however, and had worked through his unpleasant karma. He had managed to repay his debts. The other souls, therefore, saw hope for themselves as our friend the Seeker had managed to fulfil *his* karma. That was why it was so important for them to make the Seeker aware that he had been working in the pyramids of north-eastern Atlantis. By doing this, they were hoping that he could help them and give them light within the darkness they had created around themselves. Edgar Cayce has written and spoken a great deal about this problem with Atlanteans who have not been able to reincarnate.

Our friend the Seeker did not ask any questions. He just received the message. He did not tell of this experience to anybody, at least not for many years. The few people to whom he did eventually reveal this story made no comment at all. Not much was to be said – they just had an empty look in their eyes…

---

*An oracle is a person or agency considered to provide wise and insightful counsel or prophetic predictions, most notably including precognition of the future, inspired by deities.

Chapter 2

The Calling of the Wounded Healer. The Three Demons

Years went by. Almost 20 years. Life had taught him many things, taken away many illusions. Wives had come and gone.

Then one day L. brought him into contact with a shaman who wanted to help the Seeker on his way. The shaman was clairvoyant and immediately told him that, before he could guide him through and into the spiritual world – before he could lead him on his spiritual travels into the higher realms of existence – our friend the Seeker had to ask for forgiveness for a great sin. He had to obtain this forgiveness from the great Mother, Nature… Natura… Demeter… the Great Dragon…

'What sin?', our friend asked. 'What sin?'

The shaman was quite clear; the Seeker had committed a huge sin, many incarnations ago. In fact, 15 lives ago – or 25,000 years ago, to be exact! At this time, the shaman told him, our friend had been entrusted with the leadership of a relatively large group of people – people that trusted him. He was an oracle in a pyramid in ancient Atlantis, at the end-times of this great and glorious continent, just before the Great Destruction. This place was in the north-eastern part of Atlantis, close to what was then the gradually emerging continent of Europe, in the area of present-day Ireland.

The sin consisted of wrongfully leading this group of people away from the heart, from true compassion – of severing the head and thinking from the heart and feeling, leaving the head and thinking to be without feeling. The Seeker had blocked off the power of the heart, thus corrupting the heart chakra.

This was done in order to gain power, in order to be able to rule over these people like a tyrant. This was the great sin, a sin towards God himself. At that time, the Seeker knew that what he was doing was sinful; he knew that it was wrong. But he also knew that it would be easy to correct this sin later on, to open the passage between the head charka and the heart chakra, after he had used these people for his own purposes. He had the power to do so. He had the power and ability to repay for his misuse of people, to straighten out his great sin. He was, after all, a great and powerful oracle.

Little did he know!

The powers that he had at the end of the Atlantean period were lost during its destruction. Using the powers he once owned as an oracle, the restoration of his karma and recompense for sin would have taken but a few years. Now it would take many lives. In fact, it took 15 lives.

He immediately understood what was being said, and the memories of the fiery experience in Ireland stood before his spiritual eyes. So, the Irish experience was important after all. In fact, it was very important.

*

Rudolf Steiner had answered a question about such a misuse of power during a lecture course on agriculture given in Koberwitz (in modern-day Poland) on 14 June 1924. Steiner had just explained how to hinder the multiplication of mice, rodents, parasites and insects. This method was described as follows:

> … And now, imagine that you do the following: You catch a fairly young mouse and skin it, so as to get the skin. There you have the skin of a fairly young mouse. (There are always enough mice, albeit they must be field-mice if you wish to make this experiment.) But you must obtain this skin of the field-mouse at a time when Venus is in the sign of Scorpio.
>
> Those people of olden times, you see, were not so stupid with their instinctive science! Now that we are passing from plants to animals, we come to the 'animal circle' — that is, the zodiac. It was not called so in a meaningless way. To attain our end within the plant world we can stop at the planetary system. For the animal world, that is not enough. There we need ideas that reckon with the surrounding sphere of the fixed stars, notably the fixed stars of the zodiac.
>
> Moreover, in the growth of plants, the Moon-influence is well-nigh sufficient to bring about the reproductive process. In the animal kingdom, on the other hand, the Moon-influence must be supported by that of Venus. Nay, for the animal kingdom the Moon influence does not need to be considered very much. For the animal kingdom conserves the lunar forces; it emancipates itself from the Moon. The Moon-force is developed in the animal kingdom even when it does not happen to be full Moon. The animal carries the force of the full Moon within it, conserves it, and so emancipates itself from limitations of time.

This does not apply to what we here have to do; it does not apply to the other planetary forces. For you must do something quite definite with the mouse-skin. At the time when Venus is in Scorpio, you obtain the skin of the mouse and burn it. Carefully collect the ash and the other constituents that remain from the burning. It will not be much, but if you have a number of mice, it is enough. You can easily get enough.

Thus you obtain your burned mouse-skin at the time when Venus is in Scorpio. And there remains, in what is thus destroyed by the fire, the corresponding negative force as against the reproductive power of the field-mouse. Take the pepper you get in this way, and sprinkle it over your fields. In some districts it may be difficult to carry out; then you can afford to do it even more homeopathically; you do not need a whole plateful.

Provided it has been led through the fire at the high conjunction of Venus and Scorpio, you will find this an excellent remedy. Henceforth, your mice will avoid the field. No doubt they are cheeky little beasts; they will soon come out again if the pepper has been so sprinkled that a few areas remain un-peppered in the neighbourhood. There they will settle down again. Undoubtedly the influence of it rays out far and wide; nevertheless, it may not have been done quite thoroughly. But the effect will certainly be radical if the same is done in the whole neighbourhood.

After this instruction Rudolf Steiner was asked the following question from one of the participants (and here our friend the Seeker started to get really interested as this touched upon his own karmic problems).

Question: Can the method given be applied to other species? I mean, to any kind of vermin? Is it permissible without further scruples to destroy animal and plant life in this way over wide areas? The method might be greatly abused. Some limit ought surely to be set, to prevent a man from spreading destruction over the world.

Answer: As to its being permissible, let us assume for a moment that such a thing was not permitted. (For the moment I will not speak of the ethical — occultly ethical — question.) If such procedures were not allowed, what I have repeatedly hinted at would inevitably follow: agriculture would go from bad to worse in civilized countries. Not only intermittent periods of local starvation or high prices would occur, but these conditions would become quite general. Such a state of affairs may well be with us in a none-too-distant future. We have thus no other choice. Either we let civilization go to rack-and-ruin on the Earth, or we must endeavour to shape things in such a way as to bring forth a new fertility. For our needs today, we really have no choice to stop and discuss whether or not such things are permissible.

Nevertheless, from another point of view, the question may still be asked; and from this aspect we should rather consider how to establish once more a kind of safety-valve against misuse. It goes without saying that when these things are generally known and applied, abuses will be possible; that is quite evident. Nevertheless, it may be pointed out that there have been epochs of civilization on the Earth when such things were known and applied in the widest sense. Yet it was possible for those among mankind who were in earnest to keep these things within such bounds that the misuse did not occur.

Abuses did indeed occur in an epoch when far graver abuses were still possible, because these forces were universally prevalent. I mean during the later periods of Atlantean evolution, when a far greater misuse occurred, leading to grave catastrophes. Generally speaking, we can only say that the custom of keeping the knowledge of these things in small circles and not allowing it to become more general, is justified; but in our times it is scarcely possible any longer. In our time knowledge cannot be retained in limited circles; such circles immediately tend in one way or another to let the knowledge out. So long as the art of printing did not exist, it was easier; and at a time when most people were unable to write, it was easier still.

Nowadays, for practically every lecture — however small the circle where you hold it — the question is immediately raised: Where shall we get a shorthand writer? I do not like to see the shorthand writer; one has to put up with them, but it would be better if they were not there (I mean the short-hand writer, not the person, needless to say).

Must we not also reckon, on the other hand, with a further necessity—namely, the moral improvement of all human life? That alone can be the panacea against abuses — the moral upliftment of human life as a whole. Admittedly, when we consider certain phenomena of our time, we might become a little pessimistic; but in regard to this question of the moral improvement of life we should never tend to a mere contemplation of facts. We should always try to have thoughts that are permeated with impulses of will. We should consider what we can really do for the moral betterment of human life in general. This can arise from spiritual science. Spiritual science will have nothing against it if a circle is formed which will act from the outset as a means of healing against possible abuses.

After all, in nature too it is so: everything good can become harmful. Think for a moment: if we had not the Moon-forces below, we could also not have them above. They simply must be there; they must be working. That which is requisite and necessary in one sphere in the highest degree, is harmful in another. That which is moral on one level is decidedly immoral on another. That which is ahrimanic in the earthly sphere is only harmful because it is in the earthly sphere. When it takes place in a realm that is but a little higher, its effect is definitely good.

As to your other question, it is quite right: the method I indicated for the nematode applies to the insect world in general. It applies to all that portion of the animal world which is characterized by the possession of an abdominal marrow and not a spinal marrow. Where there is spinal marrow, you must first skin the animal. In the other case, the whole creature should be burned.

Our friend the Seeker pondered over these questions and answers for a long time, and they lay there in his consciousness whilst he was talking to the shaman and considering his great sins. However, the Seeker was ready to continue his venture into the unknown.

'I need to know more about this', he said to the shaman, for he sensed that it was important to find out all possible details.

'I can try to take you, to lead you back to this time', the shaman said:

> I will give you a shamanistic drink called ayahuasca which opens your mind to see, experience and understand this time, this life of yours, this action of your great sin. You see, all memories of all lives are stored in your mind, in what is called the Akashic Record. This is a record that is made and stored in the etheric realm of the world, where all the deeds of every person who has ever existed are written down, imprinted. It contains everything that has ever happened. To give you access to this record, I will give you a drink called ayahuasca. This drink contains DMT, the same substance that is released from the brain at the moment of death. When one dies, the memory is set free, and you recall all that has happened. People that have almost died can tell you about this experience. They experience seeing their whole life, everything that has ever happened to them and all that they have done, in a huge panorama. After some time, if the dying person does not come back to life, she or he will also remember all former lives, all that has happened for thousands of years.

The Shaman went on:

> Come to me in two months' time. You need this time to prepare for the journey, this spiritual event. On the day of the journey you must not eat, and in the evening I will give you the shamanistic drink.

What is ayahuasca?

People who have consumed ayahuasca report having spiritual revelations regarding their purpose on Earth, the true nature of the universe as well as deep insights into how to be the best person they can be. This is viewed by many as a spiritual awakening and what is often described as a rebirth. In addition, it is often reported that individuals feel they gain access to higher spiritual dimensions and make contact with various spiritual or extra-dimensional beings who can act as guides or healers. Author Don Jose Campos claims that people may experience profound positive life changes subsequent to consuming ayahuasca.

Vomiting can follow ingestion; this purging is considered by many shamans and experienced users of ayahuasca to be an essential part of the experience, as it represents the release of negative energy and emotions built up over the course of one's life. Others report purging in the form of nausea, diarrhoea and hot/cold flushes.

The ingestion of ayahuasca can also cause significant, but temporary, emotional and psychological distress (the 'bad trip'). Long-term negative effects are unknown. However, very few deaths due directly to participation in the consumption of ayahuasca have been reported. The deaths may be due to pre-existing heart conditions, as ayahuasca may increase pulse rates and blood pressure, or interaction with other medicines taken, such as antidepressants, and in some cases possibly a result of the addition of the hallucinogen brugmansia in the brew.

Role of shamans

Some shamans and experienced users of ayahuasca advise against consuming it when not in the presence of one or several well-trained shamans. In some areas there are purported brujos (wizards) who masquerade as real shamans and who entice tourists to drink ayahuasca in their presence. Shamans believe one of the purposes for this is to steal one's energy and/or power, of which they believe every person has a stockpile.

The day of the drinking of the ayahuasca had arrived. The Seeker sat in the house of the shaman. He was given a cup of the prepared mixture, and by drinking the content he became connected to the spirit of the plants.

First, he felt nothing. Then, suddenly, he was transported out of his body. It was not unlike the experience he had felt with the fire in Ireland a long time ago. In a way, he died. He liberated himself from his body and floated upwards. It was as if he could fly... actually it was not 'as if'... Indeed, he *could* fly!

He flew in spirit, traversing time and space, to the old continent of Atlantis. There he incarnated as a bird, like a modern-day parrot, huge and with bright colours. He sat in a tree, and then found that he could also fly. He was flying like a bird between the trees. He *was* a bird. He went *de facto* into the body of a bird, and could see from its eyes himself – not from outside – having now both wings and a beak.

He became aware that it was quite difficult to eat without hands, but after a while he managed to use his beak like other birds.

This experience was so full of joy and light that he delighted in being a bird for almost two hours.

Then he came to realize that he was not actually in ancient Atlantis, but in modern-day South America, in the state of Amazonas (Brazil). The old demons and spirits that had committed their bad deeds in ancient Atlantis, hindering them from participating in world development, had today taken refuge in South America.

After two hours of such joy, he remembered his mission, or maybe the shaman reminded him of his purpose – of what he was actually there to do. He started to float upwards in the air; up, up to the higher spiritual realms… and then back in time.

When he reached his incarnation as an oracle, he experienced something unexpected… He met three dangerous and extremely strong demons. Before he could access the details of this particular incarnation where he had committed his huge sin – where he had separated the head and heart of his entrusted peoples – he had to overcome this demonic obstacle. And this was not a small challenge, not by any means! Later, he came to understand that these demons actually *were the sins* he had committed in ancient Atlantis.

These demons were huge, fierce and strong. He saw and understood that they had been with him for 25,000 years. They had been with him in all his destructive ways of being, in all his ill deeds. He had created them in his incarnation as an oracle; created or attracted them from another dimension, from another realm of existence. These demons had been with him throughout his many lives, and had helped him in his greed for power, in his black deeds, in his manipulations of others, in his misuse of all that he could misuse…

'What do you want with us?', they shouted at him. Their voices felt like thunder. 'I want us, both you and me, to be free', answered the Seeker calmly. 'We have followed the black path together long enough. Now the time has come to change. The time has come to end this. Now the time has come to choose the white path. Now the time has come to make all the old, dark karma into good karma. Now it is time to refrain from power.'

He was quite amazed with himself and his great boldness; how he could say all this when confronted with such terrible and frightening creatures. And in a split second he understood much of his own life:

- Why he had always avoided situations that would have given him power over others.

- How he had refrained from being chosen to be a representative for classes at school.
- How he had refused leadership in organizations relating to his work.
- Why he had travelled the whole world to teach colleagues to diagnose with their heart and not with their head.
- How he had explained in all his lectures that truth could never be found solely through thinking.
- Why the forces of the heart had to be considered, and not only the head.

Suddenly, his whole life had meaning; everything fell into place.

He understood that he had to fight* the demons. He had to fight them with the mental projection of his earthly soul, expressing itself in his material body; he had to fight them with the whole of his soul. This was because the memories and actions committed in previous ages and past incarnations were still currently imprinted in his soul and expressed in his material body. Now, in this present incarnation, he had to use his 'muscles and arms' to fight them, even though he knew that this was only an illusion, for there are no actual 'muscles and arms' in the spiritual world. Still, he had to fight as if he were in the material world (much like in the film *The Matrix*).

The fight with the demons was set in motion. It was as if it were a real battle, a fight that required strength and needed muscle. (It must be repeated, however, that the 'muscles' required were not material as in the ordinary physical world, but *spiritual* muscles that appeared to be physical – and actually may be characterized as physical – which is not equivalent to material.**)

The Demons offered strong and fierce resistance, but the Seeker knew that he had to get *past* them; he had to *go through* them. Yes, he understood and realized that in overcoming the demons he had actually *to pass through them*.

He had much experience in this 'going through' from his work with horses and pulse diagnosis. When he diagnosed animals through the

---

*The expression 'fight' is not really appropriate in this context and does not point to the true meaning of this particular situation. Rather, one is speaking of a forced and willed transformation of the demons – that is, the old sins – that had to take place.

**In spiritual science a definite distinction is made between 'physical' and 'material'. This distinction may be difficult to understand, but the concept is nevertheless used in this book.

pulse, he actually went into the body of the animal with his conscious-ness, all the way to the middle of the heart, through all the twelve energetic layers of the body.* 'So, this training also had some impor-tance and meaning in my life', he thought.

Later, the Seeker told me that one of his very early experiences had helped him understand the importance of 'going through', or '*not* going through', spiritual entities. He had experienced this in a meeting with a tree spirit, when he was working as a shepherd during the summer in the Dovre mountains of Norway at the age of 21. Two days after his birthday, this important and momentous understanding dawned on him.**

Here is a short quote from the book *Poplar*, where the Seeker's expe-riences with trees are described:

> Then Poplar spoke – I still do not know what exactly he said. His words floated into my mind as a quiet stream. I answered, or asked. He explained, or spoke. I do not know for how long he spoke. At the end I stood there, and it all was over. Eve-ning had come. It must have lasted for several hours. I do not know more. However, I was absolutely conscious about what he said, what he told me. He told me the same thing in many different ways. His message was that I 'must not pass through him', that I 'must not go through him'. He was quite clear about this; that I must not 'go through or pass him'. I had to stop in front of him and face him, face to face… I have pondered upon this message many times, and given it much thought… A long time passed before I got the faintest understanding of what he might have meant. Never again did he speak to me in such a direct way as he did. It was a one-time experience. But the message was clear. Maybe later in my life I would understand.

Today our friend the Seeker understood what the tree named Poplar had meant. If you go through a spirit, you change it or kill it (as in the film *The Matrix*, at the end of Part 3). If the spirit is friendly or bene-ficial, you must never *go through* it. This knowledge is very deep and mysterious.

---

*This is described in the book *7-fold Way to Therapy* (CreateSpace Independent Publishing Platform, 2015).
**This is described in the book *Poplar* – a book about talking with trees (Cre-ateSpace Independent Publishing Platform, 2015).

He knew he had to *go through* the demons, however, and get to the other side. On the other side he knew 'the light' was waiting for him; the people that trusted him were waiting, at the end of the long, long path of evil…

He became more and more tired. He could not rest for one moment or else the demons would get the upper hand. They were impossible to go through. In a split second he felt despair, but this despair brought with it salvation. He understood that strength and power could not bring him victory. He understood that *Love* was the only way… The power of the heart.

He called out for Christ, the love and light of Christ… and in the same instant the demons were noticeably weakened… This was a very important moment, but he did not understand or conceive the full importance of his own cry. He had to concentrate all his strength on conquering the demons.

They showed definite signs of weakening, and the darkness faded. He suddenly felt a glimmer of hope, and faith entered his spirit. Victory was approaching. After a final effort he really managed to *go through* the demons – straight through… and out into the light. A door opened, leading on to a balcony. He went outside. There, gathered at the base of a pyramid, in which the fight had been fought, stood all the people. His people.

They hailed him. The victory was won. Yet still he had not seen or come to know how he had hurt his people; how he had closed the hearts of the ones that were dependent on him. There was still more to do.

He fell asleep and slept soundly until morning – late morning.

Further considerations

The fight with the demons later proved to be a very important moment and experience for him. He had been prepared for this fight during his whole life, through many trials and many errors. Not only had he been prepared for this fight, but the fight itself had huge implications, resulting in knowledge that he would use for the rest of his life. It was both an end and a beginning.

Firstly, he learned of – or rather began to understand – the power of Christ. This insight had dawned upon him over a very long period of time; he had travelled a long path to understand this deep secret. He had probably used many lives.

Throughout his life he had felt a deep admiration for Christ, for Jesus. Even when he was in his teens, thinking and believing that he was an atheist, he often felt tears starting to flow when he heard stories about Jesus Christ – even if only His name was mentioned. This caused problems when he was with his friends, who did not share the same feelings but instead showed tendencies towards blasphemy.

Later in life he wanted to honour Christ by creating a big golden cross and placing a deep red ruby in the middle, right at the crossing point. This he did, but after some years it was stolen. Not forgetting his intentions, he made a new cross with another large red ruby set in the middle, and this now hangs around his neck, always.

When C. and A., who we will meet later, described the knife he had killed them with, he recognized this cross. It was the dagger transformed into the future sword, formed as a cross (as described in the Biblical 'Revelation of St John').

He had now chosen the white path, where the ruby-ornamented dagger had transformed into a ruby-ornamented cross.

Secondly, he learned to 'see' demons and demonic structures, especially those with a pathological effect on humans and animals. This ability developed over the years to come. A great step forward in this development occurred later, when he met A. and was able to penetrate much deeper into the past, beyond that fatal incarnation 25,000 years ago… although he could not tell exactly how far.

This 'seeing the demons' would become an important aspect in his work with healing, in using medicinal plants and generally in understanding the cause and treatment of disease* and developing medical abilities which Rudolf Steiner refers to or characterizes as 'Hygienic Occultism'.**

Rudolf Steiner once commented that his spirit would always follow, help or be connected to all those who had read his books, heard his lectures or in some way been connected to him. He would be attached to them in all future incarnations, for all eternity. This is how and why a connection to the teachings of a highly developed spiritual teacher can work wonders for an individual. Bearing this in mind, how much more valuable would it be to connect to the teaching of Christ – to the being of Christ?

---

*This is partly described in the book *7-fold Way to Therapy* (op. cit.).
**This is further described in my forthcoming book *The Northern Way of Initiation*.

Chapter 3

Memories are Returning. Meeting C. The End of the Demonic Karma. Meeting H.

Two more years went by.

He had been working with the understanding of what the three demons had meant to him, how they had corrupted him, how they had led him astray; even more, how *he* had used the demons to strengthen and support his lust for power and pave his way towards evil.

He worked continuously on how to free himself from his old karma, from his link to the demons, and how to become a better human being. He also worked deeper on understanding how he could utilize his new understanding of the way demons work in human beings, and how the consciousness of Christ can counteract the dominion of evil, of disease itself. He tried to understand this through his work with patients, both animals and humans.

Slowly he felt that gradually he became freer from the darkness in his mind.

One day he sat talking to his daughter, E., who was also a veterinarian, working in his home area. All of a sudden, he noticed a change in her. She changed before his very eyes. It was as if she had been blessed with healing powers – as if the power emanating from her hands had become stronger. Not wanting to embarrass her he did not say anything.

Then something unexpected happened. After a period of silence, she said to him: 'Dad, it is quite strange… It is as if my healing power has increased. The last patients I treated healed faster, stronger and more thoroughly than before.'

It was strange that both of them, sychronistically, perceived, thought and expressed the same thing at the same time. Coincidence you might say, or perhaps telepathic communication? Not much to ponder on its own, something soon forgotten… had something else not happened.

This 'something else' happened just a week later, when a very interesting and synchronistic revelation occurred that connects this small incident with the main story of this book. The Seeker was in Germany presenting a course on veterinary medicine. After the course, C. came up to him (he did not know her), and asked for a conversation. 'Yes, I have a few minutes just now', he answered. She said that she needed some time to tell what was on her mind, so after the course they walked together along the shores of the nearby lake.

C. told the following story: (Be aware that she knew nothing of his former encounter with the demons, his dark karma, his past life – lives – in Atlantis, or what had changed in the healing abilities of his daughter just a week earlier.)

'A long, long time ago you were connected to some demons', she told him.

> This connection was based on your misuse of magic, your greed for power and your lust for ruling over people. After this had gone on for many thousands of years, 'the White Board' (the Masters) in the spiritual world decided to take away your powers and keep them hidden until you had changed. This happened about 4,000 years ago.* You were at that time – in that life – living in China. You practised medicine combined with black magic and used your power within the community. You were also very high up in the Chinese hierarchical system. In that life I was married to you. I too practised magic, although not the black version. I agreed to the taking away of your powers. I even helped in doing so. Your mother, who also knew magic, and I were the main people concerned in the taking away of your powers. Your mother at that time was the same entity as your mother in this life, which is why you have had your challenges and problems. Because I helped to take away your powers, you killed me, along with your mother.**

After thinking for a short while, she continued: 'You stabbed me with a huge dagger, ornamented with a big ruby on the shaft.' A certain sorrow or melancholy came over her face. 'I loved you so much and you killed me. I have had problems excusing you for that. It was not necessary at all. We could have solved that problem; it was, after all, done to protect you from yourself.'

The mentioning of the dagger made a deep impression on him, for throughout his life he had felt a deep longing and fascination for ruby-ornamented crosses and knives. He had, as mentioned earlier, made himself a golden cross with a ruby in the middle. Also for many

---

*This incarnation is described in my book *The Lucifer Deception* (Clairview Books, 2020).

**The latter is not mentioned in *The Lucifer Deception*. This is because my mother's killing is not within my personal memory, but was told to me.

years he had practised the Rose Cross Meditation, where one can reach the spiritual world by going through a dark cross with a circle of red roses at its the centre. The roses in the middle of the cross have a close resemblance to rubies or drops of blood.

After a while she continued:

> Now, in this present life, the 'Masters of Destiny' ('the Celestial Board') have seen that you have chosen the white path, and decided that the powers you had 4,000 years ago will be given back to you. Some of the powers have already been given to you, but most of the remaining powers have been given to your daughter, and this happened a week ago. Did you feel something happening to her a week ago?

He was amazed at this!

> More powers will be given to you when you have freed yourself completely from the demons, paid back your sins to *all* of the people that you have destroyed, and restored your karma.

He was stunned, astounded… A poem, or rather the text of a song that he had composed when he was 21-years-old, appeared in his mind:

> Oh, I thought you had passed
> but you caught me at last
> I know I could never have won
>
> but I wish that I had
> cause I'm feeling so sad
> that I lost the girl of my own
>
> may your thoughts be all damned
> may you live in the hell
> that you speak of to me
>
> and leave to the man
> all the stars that you hide
> and *all the people that you destroy.*

It struck him that, even at the age of 21, he had been involved with destructive actions in his lust for power, and had destroyed many destinies.

C. also told him that the three demons he was still connected to had a strong hold on her, on her children and on her husband. It was of crucial importance to their whole family that he succeeded in his life's mission – to defeat the demons and transform them into light and love, and to free himself from the karma he had manifested in his greed for power 25,000 years ago.

He knew his struggle was not yet over.

*

Two months later, the Seeker was lecturing in the northern part of the USA, close to the Canadian border. For an excursion during the course, the group visited an Amish farming community that used only hand-tools and horse power. Electricity was not allowed within the community. Whilst they were walking around, the Seeker happened to stand next to H.* Together they were looking at one of the Amish horses, and they both saw clearly that the horse was in pain. The Seeker then concentrated on healing the horse, finding out which process was deficient and where the origin of the problem was. He then treated the horse through intensified concentration on an acupuncture point.

The treatment worked very well. The horse indicated clearly that the pain had disappeared. Then in amazement H. turned to him and asked: 'How do you know my name?'

'I do not know your name', he replied.

'But you shouted my name, you called me, just at the moment when the horse was healed', she said. Something then happened between the two of them; something floated between them, something balanced out into eternity.

---

*The Seeker had often thought about the use of electricity and how it might influence the spiritual world. Rudolf Steiner said that material energy forms like electricity belong to the Eighth Sphere, which consists of materialized spirituality, seized by the dark forces. We have four kinds of etheric energy: life-ether, light-ether, warmth-ether and chemical-ether. Electricity is the materialized light-ether seized by Ahriman. Magnetism is the materialized chemical ether, seized by Lucifer. Atomic energy (or perhaps rather vacuum-energy) is the materialized life-ether seized by the Asuras. The Seeker had always considered such energy-forms as necessary, but when he observed the elemental beings present at the Amish farm, he began to have doubts. He had never seen such joy and happiness in the faces of elemental beings.

A few nights later he woke up around 3 am. He was not inside his body. He had excarnated and had entered the spiritual world, and there he floated. This was not new to him. He had experienced this before.

He stood in front of a Celestial Board. The leader of the Board addressed him saying: 'She was the last one. The last one you had to repay. Your karma is resolved. Now you are free.'

What are elemental beings?

Elemental beings are the living entities we meet or find in the elemental world. This world is the closest 'spiritual' world to our material world. This elemental world is the spiritual foundation of materiality, and as materiality is hidden behind three veils, the elemental world is thus threefold. The third elemental realm *is what most clairvoyants describe, containing the form of all nature-beings. This realm is created through cooperation between the angels and luciferic beings.* The second elemental realm *is unknown to most clairvoyants, and contains the foundation of all different atoms. This realm is created through cooperation between the archangels and ahrimanic beings.* The first elementary realm *is inhabited by the beings of cosmic vacuum, and they cannot be seen. This realm is created through cooperation between the archai and azuric beings.*

The first elementary realm:

The first elementary realm is the realm of brilliant colours, the first state of life that each of the seven major planetary stages of world development (old Saturn, old Sun, old Moon, Earth, new Jupiter, new Venus, future Vulcan) goes through in the course of its development. Each state of life is further subdivided into seven states of form.

Rudolf Steiner reports: 'The first elementary realm is difficult to describe. To imagine this realm we may first grasp the thought of a spiral, then the thought of a lemniscate. Now put yourself within the intention before the form emerged, that is, first within the intention of the spiral and then within the intention of the lemniscate. Imagine a world filled with such thought germs. This formless world is the first elementary realm.'

---

*Lecture of 27 October 1905, *Foundations of Esotericism* (GA 93a).

The second elementary realm:

> The second elementary realm is the realm of 'free tones'. This realm
> is the second state of life that each of the seven major planetary
> stages of world development goes through in the course of its devel-
> opment. Each state of life is further subdivided into seven states of
> form.

This realm also relates to inspiration, the archangelic realm,
the second angelic hierarchy and the forces of the Son (Christ).

> Rudolf Steiner states: 'The tones that permeate the room are
> ordered by numbers. What is particularly worth considering is
> that from the beginning, from the outset, things were in a certain
> way, in certain relationships. One figure could act on another in
> such a way that it did not hurt it, or in such a way that it made it
> disperse. That was called the measure of things. Everything was
> ordered by measure, number, shape. Think away the sensory qual-
> ities, and you will perceive the world filled only with such figures
> of thought. That is the second elementary realm. That is the basis
> of the third. We only have forms that are woven by thoughts, the
> world etheric thought.'*

The Third elementary realm:

> The third elementary realm, the realm of coloured forms, is the
> third state of life that each of the seven major planetary stages of
> world development (Old Saturn to Vulcan) goes through in the
> course of its development.

This realm also relates to imagination, the angelic realm,
the third angelic hierarchy and the forces of the holy spirit.

> Steiner says: 'Imagine a world in which only the perceptual
> qualities flow through space and are not perceived in certain forms.
> Think coloured clouds running through the world, sounds through
> the world, all our sensations fill the space without being tied to a
> form: then you have the third realm of the elementary world; these
> are the elements of light and fire, penetrating the space. Even in the
> astral realm, man is a coloured cloud. We now want to go a little
> further. When we see a thought form, it is such a coloured cloud,

---

*Ibid.

	Form of entities - numbers	Earthly structures and rhythms	Top-bottom movement	Imagination	feel	Lucifer	Angels	Third angelic hierarchy	natural substances molecules
Third elemental realm	Form of entities - numbers	Earthly structures and rhythms	Top-bottom movement	Imagination	feel	Lucifer	Angels	Third angelic hierarchy	natural substances molecules
Second elemental realm	Atom Structure – weight	Planetary rhythms	Right-left movement	Inspiration	think	Ahriman	Archangels	Second angelic hierarchy	atoms metals
First elemental realm	Force or dull fabric – measure	Cosmic structure	Front-back movement	Intuition	will	Azuras	Archai	First angelic hierarchy	vacuum

a vibrating movement. If you want to generate a thought, you have to draw the figure in question into the astral space. This is what magicians do; they draw the shapes into space and then surround them with astral matter. You then conduct astral matter along the figure. The third realm of the elementary is not irregular, but a whirring in such lines, everything is an expression of beautiful forms that have luminosity in themselves. They are like luminous bodies that float through the space, shining from the inside."

The four elements and the nature beings are contained in the third elementary realm, the realm which people know the best (very few have experienced the second and the first realm). (At this point, the Seeker only knew the third elemental realm, so his story relates only to this realm.)

There are four basic elements of nature: fire, air, earth and water. Within each of these four elements are nature spirits *that are the spiritual essence of that element. They are made up of etheric substance that is unique and specific to their particular element. They are living entities oftentimes resembling humans in shape but inhabiting a world of their own.*

The beings in the Elemental Kingdom work primarily on the mental plane and are known as 'builders of form'.

Their specialty is translating thought-forms into physical forms by transforming mental patterns into etheric and then physical patterns. Each of them is a specialist in creating some specific form, whether it be an electron or interstellar space.

Elementals range in size from smaller than an electron to vaster than galactic space. Like the angels, elemental beings begin their evolution as small entities and increase their size as they evolve.

The elementals serving on planet Earth materialize whatever they pick up from the thoughts and feelings of mankind. This relationship was intended to facilitate the re-manifestation of 'heaven on Earth'. They take their orders from the Devas. *They do not remain individualized, as humans are. These beings are animated by the thought power of the lower angels and thus are thought forms of sorts. They may be etheric thought forms, yet they have etheric 'flesh, blood, and bones'.*

---

*Ibid.

They live, propagate offspring, eat, talk, act and sleep. They cannot be destroyed by material elements such as fire, air, earth and water because they are etheric in nature. They are not immortal. When their work is finished they are absorbed back into the ocean of spirit. They do live a very long time – 300 to 1,000 years. They have the power to change their size and appearance almost at will. They cannot, however, change elements.

Earth – Gnomes

The nature spirits of the earth are called gnomes. Subgroups include brownies, dryads, durdalis, earth spirits, elves, hamadryads, pans, pygmies, sylvestres and satyrs. The nature spirits who serve at the physical level are called gnomes. Billions of gnomes tend the earth through the cycles of the four seasons and see to it that all living things are supplied with their daily needs. *They also process the waste and by-products that are an inevitable part of our everyday existence and purge the earth of poisons and pollutants that are dangerous to the physical bodies of man, animal and plant life—including toxic wastes, industrial effluvia, pesticides, acid rain, nuclear radiation and every other abuse of the earth.*

On the spiritual level, the gnomes have an even more burdensome chore. They must clean up the imprints of mankind's discord and negativity that remain at energetic levels in the earth. War, murder, rape, child abuse, the senseless killing and torture of animals, profit-seeking at the expense of the environment, as well as hatred, anger, discord, gossip—all these create an accumulation of negatively-charged energy that becomes a weight on the earth body and on the nature spirits.

Fire – Salamanders

The Salamanders are the spirits of fire. Without these beings, fire could not exist. You cannot light a match without a salamander being present. There are many families of salamanders, differing in size, appearance and dignity. Some people have seen them as small balls of light, but most commonly they are perceived as being lizard-like in shape and about a foot or more in length.

The salamanders are considered the strongest and most powerful of all the elementals. Their ruler is a magnificent flaming being called Djin. Those who have seen him say that he is terrible yet awe-inspiring in appearance. Salamanders have the ability to extend their size or diminish it, as required. If you ever need to light a campfire in the wilderness, call the salamanders and they will help you. It has also been said that salamanders (and the other elemental beings) can be mischievous at times. For example, a fiery temper and inharmonious conditions in a person's home can cause these beings to make trouble. They are like children in that they don't fully understand the results of their actions.

They are greatly affected, as are all nature spirits, by mankind's thinking.

Air – Sylphs

The sylphs are spirits of the air. Their element has the highest vibratory rate of the four. They live for hundreds of years, often reaching over a thousand, and yet never seeming to get old. They are said to live on the tops of mountains. The leader of the sylphs is a being called Paralda, who is said to dwell on the highest mountain on Earth. Sylphs often assume human form but only for short periods of time. They vary in size from being as large as a human to something much smaller. They are volatile and changeable. The winds are their particular vehicle.

Sylphs work through the gases and ethers of the Earth and are kindly toward humans. They are usually seen with wings, looking like cherubs or fairies. Because of their connection to air, which is associated with the mental aspect, one of their functions is to help humans receive inspiration.

The sylphs are drawn to those who use their minds, particularly those involved with creative arts.

Water – Undines

The undines are elemental beings that compose water. To a great degree, they are able to control the course and function of the water element. Etheric in nature, they exist within water itself, and this is why they can't be seen with normal physical vision. These beings are beautiful to look at and are very graceful. They are often seen riding the waves of the ocean. They can also be found in rocky pools and in marshlands. They are clothed in a shimmery substance looking like water but shining with all the colours of the sea, with green predominating. The concept of the mermaid is connected with these elemental beings. The undines also work with plants that grow underwater and with the motion of water. Some undines inhabit waterfalls whilst others live in rivers and lakes. Every fountain has its nymph. Every ocean has its Oceanids.

The undines closely resemble humans in appearance and size, except for those inhabiting smaller streams and ponds. They often live in coral caves under the ocean or on the shores of lakes or banks of rivers. Smaller undines live under lily pads. Undines work with the vital essences and liquids of plants, animals and human beings. They are present in everything containing water. There are many families of undines.

The ruler of the undines is a being called Necksa. The undines love, serve and honour her unceasingly. They are emotional beings, very friendly and open to being of service to humans.

Smaller undines are often seen as winged beings that people have mistakenly called fairies. Those winged beings are seen near flowers that grow in watery areas. They have gossamer wings and gossamer clothing. Subgroups include limoniades, mermaids, naiads, oceanid, oreads, potamides, sea maids and water spirits.

Chapter 4

The Betrayal. The Closing of the Way

He met another shaman, this one came from Africa.

The African shaman also worked with plant spirits using similar methods to the first, whose knowledge came from South America. The first shaman had used the help of plant spirits from the Amazonian jungle, whilst the second used the help of tree spirits that lived in the rain forests of middle Africa.

The plant-spirits from South America were connected to the ayahuasca brew, an ancient recipe that held the keys to the Akashic Record. By drinking this bitter concoction, the participant can be given entry to the Akashic Record in such a way that they really *experience* their personal history.

What is the Akashic Record?

Akasha is a Sanskrit word meaning 'sky', 'space', 'luminous' or 'ether'. It entered the language of theosophy through H. P. Blavatsky (1831–1891), who characterized it as a sort of life force; she also referred to 'indestructible tablets of the astral light', recording both the past and future of human thought and action, but she did not use the term 'Akashic'. The notion of an Akashic Record is attributed to Alfred Percy Sinnett, who, in his book Esoteric Buddhism *(1884), wrote of a Buddhist belief in 'a permanency of records in the Akasha' and 'the potential capacity of man to read the same'. With C. W. Leadbeater's* Clairvoyance *(1899) the association of the term with the idea was complete, and he identified the Akashic Record by name, as something a clairvoyant could read. According to Marshal McKusick, former professor of Anthropology at the University of Iowa, the term Akashic Record as such was created by Rudolf Steiner.*

Accounts of purported Akashic access

Readings of the Akashic Record were central to theosophical writings, but also appear in writings of other related figures.

Among the former, Leadbeater's book Man: How, Whence, and Whither?, *claims to record the history of Atlantis and other civilizations as well as the future society of Earth in the 28th century. Rudolf Steiner referred to the Akashic Records and reported about Atlantis, Lemuria, the evolution of man and Earth, and so on.*

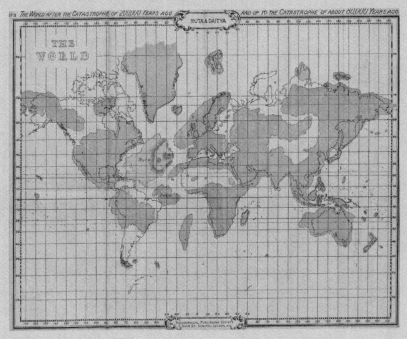

From William Scott-Elliot's The Story of Atlantis *(1896)*

This second Shaman used the roots of iboga, an African tree. The effect of this is quite different from ayahuasca, although under the guidance of experienced shamans both substances enable entry to the Akashic Record. The iboga differs in that, instead of being enmeshed in the experience, the participant has clarity of vision from pure observation and consideration.

The African shaman said much the same as the South American shaman, that the Seeker should prepare for some months, follow a special diet and not eat on the day of the ceremony. Then, he was ready to take the iboga.

What is Iboga?

The iboga tree is the central pillar of the Bwiti spiritual practice of West-Central Africa, mainly Gabon, Cameroon and the Republic of the Congo, which uses the alkaloid-containing roots of the plant in a number of ceremonies. Iboga is taken in massive doses by initiates of this spiritual practice, and on a more regular basis is eaten in smaller doses in connection with rituals and tribal dances, which are usually performed at night. Bwitists have been subject to persecution by Catholic missionaries, who to this day are thoroughly opposed to the growing spiritual practice of Bwiti. Léon M'ba, before becoming the first President of Gabon in 1960, defended the Bwiti religion and the use of iboga in French colonial courts. On 6 June 2000, the Council of Ministers of the Republic of Gabon declared Tabernanthe iboga to be a national treasure.

The day arrived, and the Seeker sat in the house of the iboga shaman. Preparations were made, the mixture was drunk, and he waited for the effect. Suddenly it was as if his sub-consciousness expanded, as if all memory and thoughts were stretched out in a never-ending line. He could see all that had happened without having to attach feelings to it – in a way it all became objective. He could see all of his lives, all that he had done, good and bad. It was as if he watched an endless road of people, landscapes, actions, causes and effects.

He directed his gaze to the old Atlantean times, fifteen lives ago – 25,000 years ago. There his sight vanished and darkness stopped him from seeing further back in time. His vision faded where his involvement with the demons had started. At that moment he understood that his work was not yet at its end.

He took a closer look at what had happened in the incarnation when he had been an oracle in the Atlantean pyramid. He saw that he had been an oracle in more than one place. There were two more mystery-centres in that area, one to the north and one further south. The northern one had to do with the education of *thinking*. The middle one, where the pyramid was situated, had to do with the mysteries of *feeling*, and southern one, the third, was dedicated to *the will*.

He saw the people who belonged to his 'congregation' – how they trusted him and how they loved him. He saw how he had hindered the energetic flow between the head and the heart of his own people. He had done this in two ways. One way was initiated by the use of magic, where he instilled some sort of tie, like a magical throat-ring,* on every single man and woman. This stopped the connection between the head chakra and the heart chakra. From this hindering 'ring' he was able to draw energy, spiritual power, which he used for his own purposes.

The other way was more physical. He literally blocked the passage between the northern centre, where his people were initiated in think-ing, from the middle pyramid-centre, where they were initiated in feeling. Between these two places he had erected an etheric/astral/physical-material fence, through which nobody could pass.

He was not able to see *how* he could draw energy from such hin-drances as rings and fences during the iboga session. The time was not yet ripe for this secret to be revealed to our friend the Seeker, but later, in this present incarnation, he was able to understand how this was achieved. (He also saw many other things which are of little relevance to this book, and will not therefore be mentioned here.)

*

The Seeker had met L. many years ago in Prague, and he knew imme-diately that he was bound to her. He also knew that he had to look after her and to pay back what he owed her. At that first meeting he had no idea what he owed her, but after they met again 20 years later, he knew exactly. She was one of his congregation 25,000 years ago, and he had been closely connected to her – more closely than most. He had bound her to him by magical means, and used her for his purposes. She felt the rings around her neck and throat many times.

This is her story:
Her tale first emerged when she was helping the Seeker to correct the grammatical errors in the book he was writing. Through constantly

---

*This method of using rings, either around the neck or around the wrist, is derived from the Atlantean mysteries. The method was common even in the Greek mysteries of the Samothracian cult. Here, this method was associated with the mysteries of the Mother Goddess, called Axieros in the ancient lan-guage, and mystically present in the rocky landscape of that island. One aspect of this cult was that the Mother of Rocks manifested her power, which was immanent in stones – in loadstones of magnetic iron – of which rings were fashioned, being made in the sanctuary itself.

going over the script, she became very aware of and in touch with the Seeker's past karma. It was very interesting to read what he had written, and she often wondered where she might fit in to this story. It was strange for her to read of other women's involvement – those who had been married and in love with the man with whom she was now living. Slight feelings of jealousy arose, which was silly as she knew the Seeker loved her deeply. However, as she continued reading over the story, these feelings subsided and she felt more and more in synch with what he was conveying. It was through this work on his book that she had an intimate revelation of something that occurred in the distant past, something that had happened around 25,000 years ago.

Living with the Seeker and his many personalities was not easy. In this life they had first met briefly, 20 years ago. Their paths had quite literally crossed in time and space, as their karmas met and destiny was fulfilled. They were together for only a few days, but the seeds were sown. Some 20 years later, she came to him for treatment and the seeds that had been sown all those years ago burst into life, blossoming and growing. They both knew that there was a deeper meaning to their meeting and the love that grew. It was as if they were living out an archetypal fairy tale. He was not an easy character and had been very intense at the beginning of their new relationship, phoning her at all hours of the day and night, cross-examining her about her thoughts and feelings on everything. She was not used to talking so much about herself and her past, and she soon realized that there were certain subjects she must stay clear of as it would lead to problems. Recognizing her own dysfunction in the relationship, she worked upon it, having had some training in the fields of effective communication. Her previous relationships had not been good, as she had always chosen men who were not worthy of her. By meeting the Seeker, she was able to unravel some of the knots that had bound, and as a consequence she felt herself expanding. Although there were tough times, the Seeker was helping her to grow. He loved her and she loved him. It was a reciprocal relationship.

The Seeker had somehow managed to attach himself to women who were 'in their heads', whereas she was based 'in her heart'. Something had opened up in her when her daughter had died – a huge change that had brought her closer to love. It was a good time for the Seeker to reconnect with her. She taught him much about the way of the heart, which he was ready to receive. He needed a love such as she was able to give and he was open. He needed a down-to-earth love, a love that was based on acceptance and forgiveness. He was at times very demanding and he needed someone like her to show him the way – someone who, when he stepped over the boundaries, would forgive him and understand him.

There were many occasions when his way of dealing with things opened up a black hole in her, which she could slip into for days. It took some years for her to develop the strength of character needed to counterbalance his. She couldn't quite put her finger on what or why things were as they were, but she knew there were power struggles lurking in the shadows. She felt this power in such a way that she began playfully to call him 'master'. But he didn't like this.

Time moved on. She understood more and more who she was actually living with, developing an inner strength and ability to deal with his overpowering ways. However, she had some secrets. One time she worked herself into a panic worrying over his reactions to something she had done. Then, something quite strange happened. She felt invisible rings coming towards the sides of her throat and clamping themselves around it, hard. She felt them physically attach themselves to her. She was chained, bound and unable to be the free spirit she was. She was under someone else's control. And then it hit her.

In his book he had written about the time that he was an oracle during ancient Atlantis, when he misused his magical powers to keep his people from connecting to the heart, and how he influenced and imprisoned them for his own personal use. One way he did this was by binding the throats of his followers with invisible magic rings – rings that, once attached, held them as his prisoner. In this way, he had them doing his bidding. He took their power and used them for his own means.

She let this feeling run through her. It was very strong and powerful and she did not for one moment doubt that it was real. What also became apparent was that, during that past time, most of the oracle's followers were unaware of the power he had over them. However, a few – like herself – had some knowledge of what he was doing to them. To free themselves from his tyranny for short periods of time, they used some sort of magic substance. He was aware of this but could not stop them. Being more powerful than them, he was still able to exert some sort of boundary – but not all the time. He was still able to inflict fear upon them, even though they achieved some mental escape.

Now it made sense. The next day, when the Seeker returned home, she told him of her experiences. She knew now that her job in this life was to free herself from his chains. It was strange because when she met him 20 years ago, he had told her of the power of rings and necklaces that could bind a person, saying that he never wore chains given as gifts because the person who gave the chain had power over the one that wore it. This stuck in her memory.

*

As time passed more memories came back to the Seeker. He considered this to be a part of the loosening of his connection with the demons. He had seen this 'remembering of the past' when he treated people with acupuncture or homeopathy; as the disease healed, the connection to the disease-creating demons also became weaker. Then those patients also began to remember more about the origin of the disease; when it started, how it started, the cause of the disease, and so on. In that way the treatment led to an enhanced understanding of the disease, and also to a change in the life-style that had led to the weakening of the different organs.

Translocation or transformation

Here it is necessary to explain a very important but mostly unknown fact about the medical treatment of both humans and animals.* There are two possible outcomes of treatment: the disease – which we might refer to as 'pathological information' or an 'adversarial' elemental being or a 'demonic structure', or simply a demon – could either *transform* or *translocate*.

A *translocation* happens in most cases of treatment – whether it be allopathic, homeopathic, acupuncture, or other forms of alternative treatment – particularly if the therapist is not aware of this possibility and treats in a certain way. To translocate the disease is usually the simplest, the most effective and easiest way to treat, and is preferred by the patient, but the disease is not changed. It translocates to another part of the body, into another form of disease or to another human being or animal. Such a translocation does not cause a spiritual development of the patient, but just relieves them of their symptoms.

---

*More developed information on this can be found in my books *Spiritual Translocation* and *Demons and Healing* (Temple Lodge 2020 and 2018).

A *transformation* happens only if the therapist is actively aware of such possibilities, and actively hinders a translocation. In this case, the therapy must be altered in a way that initiates a spiritual transformation. This way of therapy takes a longer time to heal than a simple translocation. The sad thing today is that therapists find the translocating form of therapy much more efficient, and thus they usually prefer this to a transformational therapy.

A true transformation happened now, as the Seeker's connection to his demons became looser and the demons themselves became weaker. The Seeker remembered more and more about how he had become attached to the demons, how he had been practising his magic and how he had 'sinned'.

The use of shamanistic plants in accessing spiritual worlds
To close this chapter, I would like to address the above question, which actually is not much discussed within spiritual circles, and even less in anthroposophical ones, as it seems that the answer is already evident, i.e. that it is not acceptable or congruent to sound spiritual development. Rudolf Steiner did not directly speak against the use of such plants, but in several places in his work he argues that every method for developing spiritual vision that does not involve the 'I' working on the astral body and the etheric body to create spiritual sense organs, is not conducive to the spiritual evolution of the human being. Such methods may even be dangerous, and could open the door for malignant demons. They could even give access to areas of the spiritual world where man is not supposed to enter. Such substances – such as shamanistic herbs – could also enable human beings to glimpse the contents of the metaphorical Pandora's Box, which are not beneficial to normal consciousness.

For my part, I will put this understanding in another way; if people are not able to navigate within the spiritual world, are unacquainted with it or don't even believe in it, then such substances can be dangerous hallucinogenics. If on the other hand they are accustomed to the spiritual world, these plants have the possibility to open portals to other worlds or to specific areas of these worlds.

I would even argue that the controlled use of such plants –under the guidance of an experienced guide or shaman – could be valuable when used responsibly and sparingly, but only in the case that you already have the ability, knowledge and strength to navigate within spiritual worlds. The plants are often so life-changing that using them once or twice within an entire lifetime might be sufficient. Others may need to take them several times, although frequent use can, in my view, create too wide an 'opening' that might be disturbing to everyday life.

Such plants do open doorways or portals into the spiritual world. These doorways are created by the spirits which are attached to or are mediated by the plants themselves. Different plant spirits open different doorways into spirit lands. Of course, such doorways go both ways so that – if you are not conscious or strong enough – spirits or even demons may enter from the other side. *This could be catastrophic.* But if you know what you are doing, and are strong enough or have an experienced guide, such plants can help to gain access to certain areas of the spiritual world that are highly beneficial and awakening to consciousness.

In the case of ayahuasca and iboga,* both open the way to the area of the spiritual world where the Akashic Record is to be found. Ayahuasca enables you to *experience* your deeds, while iboga stretches out the entire Akashic Record so that you can *see* everything you have done. You can see the consequences of your actions, the effect they have had on others, how your actions may have hurt your children, partners or friends. You see it all in such a way that you receive a strong impulse to make amends and do better; to repay all the people that you have hurt and to change your life in such a way that you don't hurt the ones you love again.

Because of such effects, iboga has a very strong impact on all addictive behaviours and has an extremely good success rate in curing drug addictions. The addict sees where he or she has failed, how they have hurt other people, and most importantly why the addiction began. In such a way, iboga gives one an experience of what takes place after one's death (as can be read in the books and lectures of Rudolf Steiner).

Thus, for many this experience is deep and life-changing.

I must emphasize that I am speaking solely about shamanistic plants. I have seen that the use of extracts or synthetically-produced substances that are contained in the plants – such as DMT or ibogaine,

---

Publisher's note: We emphasize that ayahuasca and iboga are illegal in many countries around the world and that use and/or possession is a criminal offence.

or LSD for that matter – have a quite different effect. In synthesizing spiritual plant substances, the ahrimanic element is drawn in. For example, with DMT the user is often drawn into the Eighth Sphere (see below), whose 'inhabitants' – according to Rudolf Steiner – are insect-like. As a result of a de-spiritualized and unconscious 'I'-function, in the Eighth Sphere these entities do not have an inner bone structure, only developing an outer structure like the chitin coating of insects.

This indicates that certain substances, foodstuffs and above all synthetic medicines and painkillers, can cause the body to connect with the Eighth Sphere. This is quite serious as these kinds of medicines are frequently used by whole populations. It can also explain why animal pellets and processed foodstuffs that are totally devoid of life, almost resembling synthetic food, act so destructively in the body, especially on the liver.

Everything that is without life, spirit and consciousness will be overtaken by the dark forces, and the same can happen with thoughts created from synthetic drugs.

What is the Eighth Sphere?

The Eighth Sphere is not a well-known concept, even amongst people with spiritual interests. For those who know what it means, it is quite a frightening idea. The Eighth Sphere is where all our ahrimanic deeds, thoughts and concepts will materialize in a planet that will be, in the far-off future, left behind by the developing universe and humanity. It is where all deeds committed without soul or consciousness will end up. It seems to me also to be a place where all our experiences with synthetic drugs, synthetic additives, medicines or food will take us. Also, our work and preoccupation within the field of computers – machines without souls – including discussions on social media, conversations through emails, and all lifeless computer interactions where the soul can't enter – all these will end up in the Eighth Sphere.

Many occultists have spoken and written about the Eighth Sphere, but there has been much disagreement and discussion about what it is, where it is and how it is organized. Some believe it is connected to our present moon, whilst some think it is beneath the Earth.

Rudolf Steiner held some lectures on this subject,[19] where he states that the Eighth Sphere belongs to our physical Earth. 'We are surrounded everywhere by the Imaginations into which the aim is that mineral materiality shall continually be drawn.' The Moon acts as a 'counteracting agent' – a place of extreme density — and this density is described by Steiner as of far denser physical-mineral character than exists anywhere on Earth. Hence Lucifer and Ahriman cannot dissolve it away into their world of Imaginations. The Moon circles the Earth as a globe of dense matter, solid and indestructible. 'When we look at the Moon, we see there in the universe a substance far more intensely mineralized, far physically denser, than exists anywhere on the Earth.'

---

*See *The Occult Movement in the Nineteenth Century*, lectures of 4 & 5 October 1915, Dornach (GA 254) and *Foundations of Esoterism*, lectures 14 & 18, October 1905, Berlin (GA93a).

Chapter 5

The New Offer of Land. The Ahrimanic Temptation

Once again, my friend the Seeker travelled to Ireland. He wanted to see and experience the places he had been to during his iboga travels, but most of all he wanted to see the place where, 22 years previously, he had seen the fire and experienced a total connection to the cosmos. He wanted to understand how he had worked there, within the pyramid. Also, in what way he had hindered and kept his people from the light, from heart consciousness.

He landed in Dublin and hired a car as he had on his previous trip all those years ago. Then he set off for the place of the fire, where the pyramid had once been. But on the way there, he suddenly changed his mind – more from an intuition than from a clear strategy. He did not go to Langford, but continued north to Sligo (the mystery-place of thinking). Here he found himself a guest house in a remote area. From there he could see both the ancient area where the old mysteries were practised, and also the old monastery of Sligo, where Christianity was first taught in Ireland – even before the founding of the monastery at Iona. Actually, it was Sligo from where the monks were sent to Iona, but that is not so relevant here. The story to be told in this book – that was investigated by our friend the Seeker – is from a much earlier time, thousands of years before.

It was the old mystery sites that interested the Seeker more than the newer Christian ones. He would only discover later that the ancient power structures connected to the old mystery sites could only be transformed through Christ consciousness (much like the treatment of disease).

The following day he drove to the old sites and immediately felt at home. The air was filled with a huge rainbow when he arrived. The rainbow was not physical; it existed in his mind and soul and in the etheric surroundings within the mystery sites of long ago. The rainbow followed him throughout the whole day.

The colours of the rainbow were like thoughts, living thoughts descending directly from the spiritual world. The different colours changed places with each other all the time, still keeping harmony. It was as if each of them called forth a new quality in the others and gave deeper meaning to the wholeness.

This rainbow had several other peculiarities, making it different from a 'normal' rainbow. In addition to the already mentioned changing around of the colours, he also observed that the colours themselves changed. The red changed from light red to a deeper red, then to violet red, to magenta, to vermilion, and so on. All the time, each single colour changed. When the colours transformed, the impression they made on him also changed radically, as if they told different stories emerging from the different colours or nuances of colours. It was like a magnificent and all-encompassing fairy tale, telling an ever-changing story – an everlasting story.

'This is how our thinking should have been', he thought to himself.*

In the area of Sligo, he found the old mystery place where he had served, or rather ruled, 25,000 years ago. It was a place dedicated to *thinking*, to spiritual thinking, as found in the rainbow that was woven into the whole area. Here, before the altar, he was able to enter the rainbow, to penetrate it and observe it from both sides. The rainbow stretched out over the entire sky, folding itself around him like a blanket – like a bowl entirely engulfing him.

He felt as he had the first time he had met the fire in Longford; he felt connected to the whole cosmos. But the connection to the cosmos was only in *thinking*. Not in *feeling*, as in Longford, and not in *the will*.

This old mystery place was constructed as a sevenfold room. Seven huge stones had been put in a circle, each representing one of the great 'time cycles' of the Earth, as well as each of the great 'incarnations' of the Earth that happened in between. The space between the huge stones was filled with memories – memories of what had happened in these time cycles, and memories of future times yet to come.

---

*This experience was probably due to the mystery-teachings performed at this sanctuary, relating to the mystery of *thinking*, and also to the third elemental realm, where this kind of colour-weaving is predominant. The mystery centre at the pyramid near Longford was related to the mystery of *feeling*, related to the second elemental realm, and the third mystery place at Rosscrea was related to the mystery of *the will*, and thus to the first realm of the elemental world. All three realms of the elemental world are in a certain respect revealed in different colours and colour qualities. More on this can be found in my forthcoming book, *The Northern Way of Initiation*.

The sanctuary at Sligo

This experience was not new to him. Apparently, this method was known by many in those ages long past: how to store information in the etheric realm which weaves between stones.

He had experienced this before whilst visiting Stonehenge in England. He had stayed in the area around the great stones for several days, trying to figure out what they meant, what they were hiding and what story they could tell. He had been disappointed with the lack of information given until he directed his spiritual gaze at the empty space *between* the stones. In these 'empty' spaces, figures and movements began to appear, long threads of cause and effect, suffering and victory... the history of all past ages, and the possibilities of all future ages. All was woven into the space between the stones.

Here in Sligo he stood gazing for a very long time. It was as if he was sucked into travelling back in time, back to unknown happenings and unknown places.

He was not afraid, as many might have been. Such 'travels' had already taken place a few times previously in his life. He had been born with a kind of epilepsy, and from a very early age had learned to excarnate. This is something that all epileptics have to learn. The nature of the disease itself is that the soul excarnates from the body.

If it goes too far, severe cramps will dominate, or else the soul may disappear totally and death would result. Our friend the Seeker did not have to experience this deep and dangerous state. He excarnated voluntarily and was then able to stop the pathological excarnation before the convulsions started. In this way he learned to master excarnation and incarnation of the soul and the spirit.

Several times he had excarnated too much, so that he had 'lost himself', and had travelled too far in both time and space. Actually, it was impossible for him to travel in both time and space at the same time. Either he travelled in time, or in space. Once he had travelled in space to the outer parameters of Mars´ orbit, far out in the planetary system. Then he had taken over an hour to come back. On another occasion he had travelled several million years back in time, and had great difficulties getting back.

One interesting feature or experience he often had when travelling like this in time or space, was that his material/physical eyes stopped functioning normally. He was no longer able to see what was around him at the time, and the images of ancient times or distant places filled his vision so totally that he actually 'saw' them as being present. Even if he physically held his eyes open, he remained at the time or place where he had travelled to. He actually saw the surroundings as if he was really there (which, in his opinion, he actually was). He firmly believed that he was there with his mind and spirit, whilst his body was in Norway in the twenty-first century.

That time when he had stood before the huge standing stones of Stonehenge, his eyes did not stop functioning. He saw the far distant epochs and places as a transparent film flickering between the stones, but was totally aware that he was physically in Stonehenge, and had not flown off to other dimensions.

*

The Seeker had visited Wiltshire in the years 2011 and 2013, in order to see for himself the stone formations, Silbury Hill and crop circles. It seemed to him that everybody he met there and with whom he discussed crop circles had a different and often personal viewpoint of what these phenomena were and how they were made. Indeed, the whole of Wiltshire, with its many standing stones and ancient constructions, seemed to be surrounded in an aura of mystery.

I will relate the Seeker's experiences in this exceptional area, as he told them to me. In the year 2011, he and his wife (L.) had hired a campervan and travelled down to Wiltshire. The first night they parked and slept in the car park at the Ridgeway, close to what is known as 'the Sanctuary', not far from Silbury Hill. There were various New Age people there together with a long row of tents and campervans. The area had the appearance of a modern-day gypsy camp.

On the other side of the fence, encircling the Ridgeway, were many old graves called the Tumulus.

That evening, as he stood looking at the Tumulus, he observed a man dressed in strange clothes on the top of the most northern area. He realized immediately that this entity was not of the material world, and asked him who he was. The entity said that he was the guardian of the Tumulus, looking after the high priest who was buried there. He had been guarding the grave for over 1,000 years.

The guardian added that he was quite tired of standing there alone as very few could see or talk to him. Our friend the Seeker asked him what or who made the crop circles, and how they materialized. He did not answer, or rather said that he did not know and did not care.

Our friend pondered on the words of the guardian and made his way to bed. Whilst sleeping he was addressed by the guardian, who was now willing to show him how a crop circle was made.* In his sleep he saw a circle being formed just outside the van. The circle was made by forces coming up from the Earth itself (from different beings of the second elemental realm (adversarial beings of ahrimanic origin), beings of the third realm (of luciferic origin) and of the first realm (of azuric origin). The whole process took only a few moments. The wheat laid itself down – in the second elemental realm a certain power over atomic structure is apparent – as if on command (it was actually commanded by the ahrimanic elemental beings).

At this moment the Seeker woke up and told his wife about the circle outside the van, describing how it looked. Then he went to sleep again. In the morning, when stepping outside the van, the circle was there on the opposite field, looking exactly as he had seen it.

---

*This is an example of how spiritual beings are often perturbed by the material body, but as soon as we are out of the body, as in sleep, they are much friendlier and more willing to communicate.

Close-up of a crop circle

Two years went by and the Seeker and his wife once again travelled to Wiltshire in search of the enigmatic crop circles. They headed for the Ridgway, expecting to find it full, but as it was now illegal to spend the night there, they were alone.

The Seeker immediately met the guardian, who was overjoyed to see him again. The guardian frolicked in delight on the top of the Tumulus.

The following night the guardian visited the Seeker and informed him what the crop circles really were, and the reason why they were being made. They were doorways, portals to the elemental world, and were mostly made by adversarial forces. The ahrimanic entities of mainly the second elemental realm, forces located in the area, had actually started to make the circles, thousands of years ago, as a means to free their master, who was imprisoned within Silbury Hill (more about this below). To counteract these attempts by evil forces, the good forces began to make their own circles. Unfortunately, human beings are not able to see the differences between the malevolent and the beneficial circles.

The guardian paused for a moment and then continued. Humans can also use the circles, but then they have to be activated in a proper way. They can only be activated by cooking a full pot of water in the exact centre of the circle, so that watery steam pours up from the centre.

The dark forces of today are occupied with seriously hindering people from experiencing the spiritual world, mainly by distracting them with material things. They are very adept in leading those interested in spiritual activities on false paths, such as misuse of drugs, sex and artificial intelligence.

The portals made by the dark forces also served another purpose – to lead people away from the heart and imprison them in the head, in the thinking. Our friend the Seeker recognized this situation, and shivered.

Then the guardian told him about Silbury Hill.

Silbury Hill (by Greg O'Beirne)

About 5,000 years ago a fierce demon haunted the lands of Wiltshire, killing people, animals and innocent children, destroying homes and leaving farms in ruins. Something had to be done. The people of the region gathered together and discussed how they could free themselves from this nightmare.

Counsel was sought from a wizard living in the western area of Britain, in Wales. He came, and he fought the demon with his powers. This fight lasted for three years, but finally the wizard was able to capture the demon in spiritual chains with the help of spells, knowledge, special stones and material that he had brought from his home region. The powers of the demon were thus imprisoned for eternity. To be sure that no person could free this monster, the wizard ordered the people to cover the demon, along with the stones and material that he had brought from his homelands, with as much soil as possible. This was done, and for generations to come the people of that region continued to bear loads of earth and limestone to stop the demon from becoming free. This is what we know today as Silbury Hill.

Nevertheless, although trapped, the demon is alive, wanting to be free, longing for the day it can re-enter the world of the living – the world of humans – to taste blood again. It can still be felt stirring in the depths of the hill, waiting for the day when Ahriman appears in physical form, for the sole purpose of fighting human individuality. Then the demon of Silbury Hill can appear in his fighting armour, and we must fight him again, this time without the wizard but with the weapons of Christ and Michael.*

Several stone rings and stone alleys were also built to keep the dark forces at bay. They were deliberately constructed to keep the dark forces *inside*, not *outside*, as many seem to believe today. Rituals were also performed to transform the dark forces.

The crop circles are primarily attempts by the servants of the dark demon to free him. However, some are made by the good forces of the Earth in order to counteract the dark forces of the Eighth Sphere – in order to keep the dark energy inside.

So, this is what the Seeker experienced in the area surrounding Silbury Hill, through reading the local Akashic Records in between the stones and listening to the stories of the guardian of the Tumulus.

*

It was late, and the chilly Irish winds started to blow. Our friend the Seeker felt tired. With much to think about, he drove wearily back to his guesthouse. The following day he was scheduled to travel further, south to Longford, to the mystery place of *feeling*.

*

The next day he drove to the site where he had seen the fire 22 years ago. He parked the car knowing nothing would happen, even though this had been one of the most important places in his life. He knew that in the spiritual world nothing happens twice, nothing repeats itself.

---

*Michael is an archangel in Judaism, Christianity and Islam.

Either you learn what you are intended to learn from the experience, or you must learn it another way. Likewise, is it impossible for two persons to experience the same thing. In the spiritual world everything is constantly new and created anew. The past can only be seen in the Akashic Record.

Our friend the Seeker entered that place in a mood of quietness and calm. There was a small country lane leading towards the place where he had experienced the spiritual fire, through fields where grazing animals stood in peace. He left the car and walked slowly over the fields towards the mystical place. Then a man – a real man this time – approached, presenting himself as the farmer and owner of this area.

The first thing the farmer said was, 'Do you want this land? I will give it to you. I am tired of running a farm in present-day Ireland; it's just work and no money. Just work and more work. Give me a couple of million euros, and I will be on my way to Bermuda.' The Seeker noted that the farmer wanted to go to Bermuda, another mystery place in this world…

This land once belonged to me, our friend thought, and now it is being offered to me again. What a strange coincidence!

'I am tired of being a farmer here in Ireland', the farmer went on. 'I want to emigrate to Bermuda.' The farmer looked the Seeker over and went away.

The farm was not well looked after. Fences were down and the road leading into the surrounding farmland was not cared for. The farmer had apparently lost interest in his farm. Maybe I should buy it, thought the Seeker, and rebuild the mystery-centre of the heart – rebuild the pyramid.

'No', said a faint voice within his heart. 'In Atlantean times these places were important for initiation; today they are without significance, except for the memories. Today the heart itself must be the mystery-place where the true Altar is built.'

He understood this message very clearly and, in understanding this deep secret, he freed himself from the earthly-material mystery place, enabling it to become cosmic and universal. This time there was no fire, just a deep feeling of completion of a destiny, the finishing of old karma.

He walked around the place. In the middle of the pastures stood a small, old stone house in ruins. He went inside. Old furniture was crushed, bottles smashed… just destruction. The cows were grazing, the sheep lay resting and chewing grass. All was peace and quiet.

As he had predicted, nothing extraordinary happened, and he soon found himself a guesthouse and slept like a baby.

*

The next day he drove further south, to the area around Roscrea, arriving in the late afternoon. This was the place where the mystery centre related to *the will* had been based. In our times, as well as in the future, the impulses from these ancient mystery places can be transformed to new mysteries with the release of elemental beings of the three elemental realms. It is possible to become a magician of the material world oneself. The *thinking*-mysteries can be transformed to what is called 'hygienic occultism'; the *feeling*-mysteries can be transformed to what is called 'mechanical occultism', and the mysteries of *the will* can be transformed to what is called 'eugenic occultism' (see below).

Third elemental realm	Up (proximal)/ Down (distal)	**Lucifer** Ahriman Azuras	number	hygienic occultism	form and individ- ual
Second elemental realm	left/right	Lucifer **Ahriman** Azuras	weight and time	mechan- ical occultism	atom and founda- tion
First ele- mental realm	front/back	Lucifer Ahriman **Azuras**	measure and eternity	eugenic occultism	vacuum and force

What are hygienic, mechanical and eugenic occultism?

To be able to work within the material realm, to master and bring salvation to material creation, we have to get to know, understand and observe the three elemental realms so that we can develop three occultisms, as follows:

- *Hygienic occultism: which deals with regulating the powers present in living beings, the beings of the third realm of creation, animals and human beings. The powers that are to be* regulated are, in particular, the luciferic forces* and the elemental beings of warmth and coldness. The only regulator is the Christ-force. This occultism belongs mainly to the third realm of the elemental world.

- *Mechanical occultism:*** is about bringing the molecular and atomic forces in resonance with the forces of both the second and third elemental realm of existence, which again can be put in action by the 'I'-force of human beings, as long as this 'I' can receive its force from Christ. This occultism belongs mainly to the second realm of the elemental world, where quantum-mechanics may also be placed, as well as the effects of homeopathy. The powers here are mediated by the elemental beings of light and darkness. The only regulator, however, is the Christ-force.
- *Eugenic occultism:* deals with the construction of the foetus, the ensoulment of the same and the incarnation of the spirit. The powers to be regulated are related to both the luciferic, asuric and the ahrimanic forces, and the elemental beings to mediate these forces are the elemental beings of life and death. This realm or force exists in the vacuum of the material world, where the elemental particles are born. Again, the only regulator is the Christ-force.

---

*The Christ forces work as a balance to the luciferic and the ahrimanic forces, and the Christ forces work in direct opposition to asuric forces. Hygienic occultism will thus need to restore the balance and find ways to oppose the asuric forces.

**Mechanical occultism is of utmost importance with regards to our future diverging paths with our ahrimanic double. We have been together for 13,000 years, or half the time of the sun's path through the zodiac. We'll continue to have a relationship for the next 13,000 years. The starting point was the Fall. The mid-point will be in the sixth post-Atlantean Cultural Age, when sexual procreation will fail (because humans will no longer reach puberty). We will be working, albeit unconsciously, with our double to prepare its future earthly vehicle – the mechanized physical body. As this progresses, our etheric body will be loosening, so that humans will become more and more detached from their physical body, eventually bequeathing it to their double. To my understanding, mechanical occultism has to do with the operation of machines through moral impulses. The moral and the mechanical must interpenetrate each other, just as light and darkness interpenetrate each other in the human being.

The Seeker was quite sure that this was the place. Standing there, he remembered how he had 'closed the way' between both the head and the heart – that is, between Sligo and Longford – and between the heart and the limbs – between Longford and Roscrea.

The closing between Sligo and Longford was done with the help of rings that were placed around the throat. These rings consisted of different metals, mainly silver and gold. The silver and the gold in the rings were under a spell – a spell able to reverse the effect of the metals; a spell that imprisoned the true forces of the metals so that they worked in an opposite direction, as all evil is turned to its opposite.[*] The silver stopped the streaming of etheric forces that needed to go from the head to the heart, while the gold stopped the forces going from the heart to the head. The streams that flowed between the heart and the limbs were not so important or strong at that time, and they were stopped by a girdle made of vines – vines containing a poison. Which poison it was he could not remember.

The closing between the heart and the limbs, between Longford and Roscrea, was much more complicated. People could go around the barriers, so in the end he used a combination of armed guards, physical hindrances and a certain spell, so that individuals who passed the barriers hallucinated and saw terrible demons and monsters. He also used real demons in this work. That was how he initially started to cooperate with demons, and how he later became bound to them. He was not afraid of cooperating with demons at that time. He had enough power to free himself later, or so he thought. How wrong he had been! It would have been much easier to break the connection with the demons if he had lost his power and ability to work magic when Atlantis had sunk into the sea. But alas, it did not work out like that…

In the end, both connections had been closed. What a crime, and what an insult he had forced upon his own people! And how much he himself had to suffer because of this.

*

Then the Seeker began to understand how and why this closing of the connection between the various parts of the body and various parts of

---

[*]The devil always sits on his horse in the opposite direction; not as in the reverse (mirror) direction as with leprechauns, but in an *opposite direction within the spiritual realm itself* – influencing matter, the material world, and leading to the Eighth Sphere.

the landscape could provide power or energy to the one in charge, in this case himself, as an oracle.

A revelation, a deep understanding, now appeared in his mind.

In this life, in the twenty-first century, our friend the Seeker had several major experiences of meeting evil. He had been confronted with situations in which evil was involved; situations where people in power, people in search of power, people that wanted power, had made rituals, constructed situations or by other means promoted relationships that enabled them to *draw* energy or power from a number of people, usually without their knowing. (And this is very close to what is called 'black magic'.) These situations involved the following:

- A secret 'political' association in Germany.*
- An osteopathic school in France.
- A religious centre in Italy.
- A spiritual organization in Europe.
- An alternative medical association in Scandinavia.
- A special psychic institute at the University of Berkeley in California.
- A castle in Germany related to the psychic institute of Berkeley.

The methods they used were always based on some spiritual/energetic procedure. It was not so important as to what kind of procedure it was; it just had to include a certain shifting or transference of energy – of spiritual energy, etheric energy. It could be a treatment with acupuncture, with homeopathy, with herbal medicine, with osteopathy, with walking in specially designed spirals, with certain connections to living beings like trees or animals, or with religious symbols or religious rituals. It could even be religious dances or speeches (as with Hitler).

The procedures or ceremonies had to be set in motion by those wanting to draw energy. They could do this from afar by using their apprentices/servants. In this way they put their intention, their will for power, their will to dominate all life into the procedure. This will or intention actually created elementary beings – and, as the intention was related to dark magic, the elemental beings became evil and

---

*The Seeker did not want to expose the names of these groups, single persons or organizations, as he feared their fury or revenge at being exposed, but he described their methods to me, in very great detail.

turned into demons. 'There are three kinds of demons', my friend the Seeker told me. He continued:

> I should know that by now. One group, the ugly ones, like the demons I had to fight, are called ahrimanic demons. They are the ones we all think about when we talk about demons. But if you read *One Thousand and One Nights*, the book of Arabic fairy tales, it describes a multitude of different demons.
>
> Another group is the luciferic demons. They are usually very beautiful, attractive and often feminine in appearance. They are described in many places, for example in Tantric Buddhism. They are often considered benign in this religion, and they help people to acquire knowledge and artistic inspiration. In the Tibetan *Book of the Dead* they are described as helping spirits in the land of the dead. They emanate a strong light, a light that almost hurts your eyes. Luciferic means exactly that, light-bearer, light-spirit, light-demons. They may lead you astray. The only salvation when confronted by them is to choose the dim and pleasant light, and not the sharp light. The dim and pleasant light leads to the Christ, and he is the only force today that can stand up to the luciferic temptation, to the luciferic light. When the Tibetan *Book of the Dead* was written, they did not have the Christ, and the luciferic powers were the only ones that could help people. The ahrimanic demons were as evil then as they are today. When meeting a luciferic spirit, many people believe it to be an angel. This can be catastrophic...

Thus explained my friend, animatedly. He continued:

> Then we have the asuric demons. They are fierce, and they are not pleasant to see. They are particularly destructive. Then we have an assortment of different demons that are derived from elemental nature beings, like the hulder, nisser or troll. Sometimes the dark forces can grab one of these entities and transform them into evil beings. In this way there are very many different types of demons in the world.

The procedures used to create demons and draw power from others are partly described in J.R.R Tolkien's *The Lord of the Rings*. Here, Sauron manages to draw energy and power from all living beings through his magic ring. Also, one should note how his will to dominate all life forms created the orchs, transforming existing elemental entities like elves into evil orchs.

The organizations mentioned above make use of such energy transference by different methods, even resorting to those described in *The Lord of the Rings*. But it is more common to do so by using the method of teaching acupuncture, herbal medicine, zone therapy and other natural healing therapies that have to do with energy manipulation of the patient. Other methods can be through creating stone labyrinths or spirals where people walk with magical symbols in their hands, or to encircle trees in order to transfer energy to the leader of the organization (or the forces behind him or her). Another method is to teach specific osteopathic procedures involving energetic changes, from which the leader or forces behind the leader can gain power.

Power gained in such a way is *always* related to the dark side, to black magic, and can never be used in a good way. Energy taken or stolen without the conscious acceptance or agreement of the one that gives it, can never be used for anything good. Power given freely, offered freely, can be used for good. That is a cosmic law, and this law can never be broken.

That is why the dark forces have so many possibilities to mislead people. The dark forces can lure, push, cheat or scare people into giving up their energy. The forces of light must always receive them as a gift, a freely given gift (see the conversation between Galadriel and Frodo in *The Lord of the Rings* where Frodo offers the Ring to Galadriel for free). And this demands that the person or persons *understand* what they do, understand and consciously take the side of the good forces of this world. The dark side does not need people who understand; they can do with the ignorant and unknowing. That is why knowledge and education is the best defence against the darkness. That is why the dark side is always against education, whether that be the education of girls, the lack of important information in schools, or the misuse of spiritual teaching.

Our friend the Seeker told me that he always felt the presence of evil as screams in the earth, or in the air. It was as if the elements themselves were screaming. Once, when he went in a stone spiral made by one of these groups, he felt the whole earth was filled with screaming and fire. It was like being in the fires of hell. In the eyes of the leaders of these organizations, he had several times seen tortured spirits, barbed wire, death, concentration camps and the fires of hell.

'This screaming is a very interesting fact', the Seeker once told me...

> Every time I meet evil materialized in a body, an entity or
> in a physical construction, I hear sounds. It might be drum-
> ming, screaming, high and unpleasant tones or music. Often
> the sounds come from the earth or from the air. When I meet
> something good or beneficial, I hear singing, angelic voices,
> harps or pleasant sounds. This is probably the origin of what
> people conceive as 'the music of the spheres', 'Angel song'
> and so on.

So, he knew very well how the evil side appeared, how evil was con-
ceived by 'spiritually hearing or seeing' human beings. He had met this
many times in his life. He had also wondered why he seemed to attract
evil and why he met the representatives of the dark side in the human
or physical world, such as the people and organizations mentioned.
None of his friends could share his experiences within this field.

Now he understood that this ability and karmic tendency to see and
face such evil came from his Atlantean incarnation as an oracle – when
he himself had been involved in dark and evil deeds. In such a way
he was able to understand the dark forces and to make a clear and
conscious decision to work against them. *Consciously to choose the good
side, the white path.*

Chapter 6

Israel and the Christ. The Dragon. Meeting A.

Half a year later, the Seeker was on a study visit to the Czech Republic (then still known as Czechoslovakia). He was attending a week-long educational course in anthroposophic medicine for doctors. There were about 200 doctors present, three veterinarians and two farriers* from Canada.

Suddenly A. stood before him. 'Where have we met before?', she asked. He remembered her at once. He had killed her many thousands of years ago – probably more than 25,000 years – with a knife that had *two* red stones as decoration.

The dagger again! This time with two red rubies. He had stabbed her under her right shoulder blade – a situation that was similar to the one concerning C., but nevertheless very different.

This meeting with A. awoke memories; memories that were so deep and far in the past that he scarcely remembered them. In the beginning he only remembered A. lying on the ground after the killing.

This distant time had always been shrouded in darkness. In his attempts to go beyond, to see what happened before the tragic incidents 25,000 years ago – incidents that chained him to the demons – he always met this impenetrable darkness. He felt the time before the catastrophe as a huge weight on his shoulders. Something beyond the darkness waited to be understood, to be explored, to be forgiven.

Now something new and unexpected unfolded within this darkness; *two small lights were to be seen*, appearing as two eyes, dark and flaming, like glowing pieces of coal. They were situated right in front of him, somewhat to his left.

He looked at A. Something new had opened up, allowing him to see the past.

'Yes, I remember you very well', he told her, 'I killed you thousands of years ago, but I could not do otherwise. I had to kill you, and afterwards I also killed myself. I did it to save us both from the darkness.' It sounded like a poor excuse.

The day after, A. was there again, standing in front of him.

---

*A blacksmith who specializes in shoeing horses.

'You did not have to kill me', she said. 'We could have found other solutions. I loved you so much, we had so much to do... yet still you killed me. Because of this I have mistrusted men all my life – and what's more, I have had a continuous pain under my right shoulder blade, just where you stabbed me.'

'I am sorry', he managed to say. It felt even emptier this time.

The next day she stood there again. 'You did not kill yourself', she said. 'You just killed the darkness in yourself. You put off the darkness and walked away, free and flowing in light. I lay there, left to my fate, dead, in darkness.'

'I am sorry', he said again, feeling totally pathetic this time. Then they parted.

Over the next days and weeks something in his memory changed in relation to this period 25,000 ago. It had been in total darkness. After the meeting with A., however, this darkness had begun to light up through two flaming dark eyes. The eyes became stronger and stronger, and after some time he could see that they were the eyes of a huge dragon. In the beginning the dragon was fierce, hostile and strong. It was impossible to come close to it, impossible to communicate with it. He felt a certain fear in addressing this huge monster, yet he continued to address it, for it stood there before his eyes constantly. He could not escape it. He had to become acquainted with this monster from the old world.

After some weeks, the dragon became noticeably less hostile. He sensed a certain recognition in her eyes – yes, he started to consider the dragon as a she, a female entity – a certain feeling, as if the dragon also remembered him. The darkness around the dragon became lighter, and light began to flow in from behind her. The light came from a point even deeper in the past. He tried to understand where the light originated, tried to get a glimpse of the source, but found it impossible. It would still take some time before he managed to do this.

The relationship to the dragon developed, and after some months she even started to smile at him. The darkness turned more and more into light, the dragon became kinder, until finally she transformed to a light-filled creature.

In this way, he accessed the deep past, more than 25,000 years ago. And the past smiled to him. Thus, the karma was transformed.

All was light.

*

The development that the Seeker experienced in meeting the dragon appears to be a cosmic rule when encountering spiritual entities of higher rank than humans. First the higher being is completely uninterested; then it starts to reveal itself, becoming friendlier. The encounter ends up in a mutual conversation.

Actually, this procedure resembles the description Rudolf Steiner gives of the process of initiation. He describes this process as a gradual development from *imagination* to *inspiration* and then to *intuition*.

In imagination one simply experiences pictures, the 'outer' images of the spiritual being. Then this imagination must fade away, must give way to the next stage of inspiration. At this stage one can speak with the spiritual entity and it reveals its intentions, its mission. At the last stage, intuition, one 'enters' the entity and becomes one with the spirit of heavenly reality.

The meeting with the dragon developed in this way. First he only saw it and there was no contact. Then the friendliness appeared and the conversation began. Lastly came the feeling that they were one.

This kind of developing knowledge of spiritual beings was quite common for the Seeker. He had experienced it previously. For example, he had been invited to go to Israel to demonstrate the effectiveness of his method for treating (and curing) cancer. Since 1984, when he first discovered and developed this new method, he had tried to convince the medical community of its usefulness. However, the echelons of modern medicine seemed to be unable to comprehend it – or maybe they were so locked in the grip of the 'demon' of the pharmaceutical companies (this demon could well be the entity known as Mammon) that they would not, or could not, listen or understand.

In Israel they wanted to try his method so, one late autumn day, he travelled by plane to Tel Aviv. Arriving at two o'clock in the morning, he managed to find a taxi. He was the only passenger, and asked to be driven to the hotel. Then something unexpected happened. Suddenly, there was a man sitting beside him in the car, on his left side. Beneficial spiritual entities always seemed to appear on the left side, whilst ahrimanic ones appeared on the right. This person was dressed as someone from 2,000 years ago, with long brown hair parted in the middle and down to his shoulders, kindly blue eyes, light skin, sandals and a bluish tunic that reached down to his ankles. The Seeker was amazed.

The man stayed with him all the time he was in Israel, and continues to be with him up to this day, only not so visible as on that first morning. In the beginning the man did not speak to him, he just looked right ahead. Then, after some weeks, he started to smile. After some months, he started to speak. In the end, our friend the Seeker felt that they were one. This meeting developed just like the meeting with the dragon. Through *imagination* to *inspiration* and then to *intuition*.

Four days after the meeting in the taxi, his Jewish friend living in Israel drove him to Jerusalem. On the way there, his friend asked him an unexpected question. 'Have you heard about the Jerusalem-syndrome?'* 'No', replied the Seeker. 'In many people, Christians, Muslims, atheists or Jews, the sight or appearance of a Jesus-like person appears at their left side. The closer they are to Jerusalem, this happens more and more frequently. If you are an atheist, you get very scared, and some are submitted to a psychiatric hospital. That is why this condition is called "The Jerusalem Syndromee"', he said.

'I have had this vision for the last four days', said the Seeker.

'That does not surprise me', replied his Jewish friend.

---

*Wikipedia says of this: 'Jerusalem syndrome is a group of mental phenomena involving the presence of either religiously-themed obsessive ideas, delusions or other psychosis-like experiences that are triggered by a visit to the city of Jerusalem. It is not endemic to one single religion or denomination but has affected Jews, Christians and Muslims of many different backgrounds. The best known, although not the most prevalent, manifestation of Jerusalem syndrome is the phenomenon whereby a person who seems previously balanced and devoid of any signs of psychopathology becomes psychotic after arriving in Jerusalem.'

Chapter 7

The Rebuilding of the Altar. The Spiritual Realm is Offered

This old story is closing now, or so it seems... and a new story begins: the story of the future building of the mysteries of *thinking*, *feeling* and *the will*, which will show in the mastering of the hygienic, mechanical and eugenic occultisms. The rebuilding of the altars. Of these three, the middle is the most important: the mystery of *feeling*.

When one becomes aware of the importance of feeling, the middle part of the soul, the sentient soul, the beginning of *sanas* (the spirit self), the middle of the three mystery-places, one becomes aware of the importance of the middle (or centre) in all relations.

This realization also started to emerge in the Seeker's treatment of patients. He became more and more aware that only 'the middle' could really disperse the disease. Treating the deficiency-related ahrimanic demons, or the excess-related luciferic demons, often just translocated the disease – the demons, the symptoms or the informational structure of the disease. In awakening or treating the middle, it is impossible to translocate the disease. One cannot really say 'treat' the middle, as the middle is not sick. The middle is not the problem. But in awakening the powers of the middle point, this will have the force to disperse and to transform the other extremes without translocating them.[*]

The long path of karma is traversed to its first stop. The old mystery places in Ireland are found and can now be restored; no longer in Ireland, but in our consciousness.

The way to the heart is opened. The passage is free. The roads are cleared and it is possible to travel. The secret of the middle is revealed. The heart is longing to bring its love to the world. His personal karma is straightened out, at least relating to what he did 25,000 years ago. Now he can concentrate on going forward and rebuilding the three mysteries – for it is time to build them again, to build them anew.

These three mysteries were built on special places in Ireland, just before the destruction of Atlantis. The consciousness of the qualities

---

[*]See my book *Spiritual Translocation* (op. cit.).

and use of the three soul forces are especially important at times of destruction, during times of change.

Our present civilization is in the process of change and is not far from destruction itself. Renewing the three mysteries is more important now than ever.

The presence of the transformed 'knife' is the salvation of this dying society. The instrument of death, which is the dagger, must be transformed to the cross, with the ruby as the rose cross. Only then can the dying culture be renewed, in the consciousness of Christ, in the practice of the middle, in understanding the *divine feeling*.

At this end-time of our civilization, the most important thing is to keep the doors open to the spiritual world. This can only be done by building upon the new mysteries; the mysteries of *thinking*, *feeling* and *the will*. And to walk the path between them.

Once, the Seeker had written a poem, as follows:

> Slowly my consciousness started to function again.
> A stream of light, an orange dawn that died.
> A waft of fragrance vibrating in departure.
> I tried to wake up.
> Memories slowly began to reveal their pain,
> Rising nauseatingly to my brain.
> Everybody that crossed my path,
> And visited my heart,
> Were wanderers like myself,
> Fulfilling their karmic necessities.
>
> The day dawned and the stars vanished like clouds.
> All roads that had been sleeping started to listen
>   for a new eternity.
> Grains of dust blew from my footprints.

Now he re-wrote the poem to read as follows:

> Slowly my consciousness stops functioning.
> The streams of light begin to become stronger again.
> The metallic smell of another reality re-emerges.
> I try to *see*.

Memories from the spiritual world vibrate slowly
        in my consciousness.
Everyone that I have ever loved touches me
        like a spring breeze.
Nobody is alien, nobody passes.
Everything said or read stands crystal clear in my mind.
The night falls and the stars shine strongly.
All roads tell me where they lead.
The dust disappears.

Postscript to Part I

What Happened to the Three Demons?

The valued reader of this book may wonder what indeed happened to the three demons. Were they sent out on a long wandering journey, ready to find another victim, another 'companion' in the human realm? No. The Seeker assured me that their transformation had begun. This transformation worked in three ways:

Firstly, they were partly changed when our friend went 'through' them during their great fight in the pyramid. This brought about a change. It freed them from their connection to evil. They became free, wandering spirits, although still ahrimanic.

Secondly, they were changed when the Seeker went to the area of the pyramid in Ireland, and in peace faced the land where they first met.

Thirdly, after this visit to Ireland, the partial restoring of his karma in meeting H. and the paying back of old debts, the demons were partly changed into beings of light. (The Seeker hoped, wrongly, that the transformation would be complete, but more of this in Part II.) To fulfil this initial process of their transformation, the demons understood that they had to die and resurrect in the Earth, with the good spirits of the Earth, the elemental beings. They had to become one with the elementals of the Earth. This would be the first step in the process of the demons' final salvation.

The demons had to die in the physical world. This was fulfilled later that autumn when they entered physical animals, possessing them. The animals then had to go through death by slaughter. This process was similar to what happened to the demons that are referred to in the Gospel of Luke, Chapter 8. Those unclean demons were forced to enter swine which then killed themselves by drowning, having jumped into a lake. The Gospel description is as follows:

> *And when he went forth to land, there met him out of the city a certain man, which had devils long time, and ware no clothes, neither abode in any house, but in the tombs. When he saw Jesus, he cried out, and fell down before him, and with a loud voice said, What have I to do with thee, Jesus, thou Son of God most high? I beseech thee, torment me not. (For he had commanded the unclean spirit to come out of the man. For oftentimes it had caught him: and he was kept bound with chains and in fetters; and he brake the bands, and*

was driven of the devil into the wilderness.) And Jesus asked him, saying, What is thy name? And he said, Legion: because many devils were entered into him. And they besought him that he would not command them to go out into the deep.

And there was there an herd of many swine feeding on the mountain: and they besought him that he would suffer them to enter into them. And he suffered them. Then went the devils out of the man, and entered into the swine: and the herd ran violently down a steep place into the lake, and were choked.

When they that fed them saw what was done, they fled, and went and told it in the city and in the country.

The Gospel says nothing about what happened to the unclean demons. The demons in the Bible story were transformed through physical death. However, ahrimanic beings cannot go through death unless they want to be transformed.

The three demons in our story wanted to be transformed, as they had been defeated and had lost their meaning in life. They had lost their human ally. In this way the demons *were* transformed; they experienced a kind of death and were reborn as spirits of the Earth, becoming earthly elemental beings. In the same way, the Christ had to go through death by entering a human being, Jesus of Nazareth, to become the Spirit of the Earth.

The demons in our tale chose to go into the sheep grazing in the fields in the vicinity, where the old pyramid once stood, at the farm of the man who wanted to sell the land to the former owner, the oracle, now our friend the Seeker. Later in the autumn, when the sheep were slaughtered, the demons were released, saved, transformed and reborn as helpers of the Earth, of the light-filled elementals working for the good.

In this way, the home of the pyramid had its final purpose in the closing off of this long story… Or so the Seeker thought…

But it was not so; this action simply enabled a transition for the demons, who became hidden from sight and could no longer be perceived, but they still existed. They were multidimensional beings, as you will see in the second part of this book.

PART II

Introduction to Part II

A Recapitulation

In the first part of this story we saw several things: how the Seeker mis-used his power 25,000 years ago, the karmic debts he had to pay, how this karma was balanced in later incarnations, and the struggle against the demons he had to face.

Many people experience the spiritual world within the astral aspect (which is the easiest to see, experience or feel). In the material world, however – also described as the third elemental realm or 'the realm of the Holy Spirit' – there are deeper and more mysterious dimensions of existence to our cosmos. In these deeper layers, where our insight and consciousness may have great difficulties to traverse, unknown realms of existence may yet be found.

One deeper layer is the elemental realm of existence – in the material world described as the second elemental realm or 'the realm of the Son' – hidden behind two veils. A further and deeper layer is the physical/material realm of existence, in the material world described as the first elemental realm, or 'the realm of the Father', hidden behind three veils.

We often think that the physical is 'just' the material, but the so-called material, in which substances have gathered and become deposited, is a strange and mighty realm of existence.

The demons described in the first section of this book were met and fought by the Seeker only in the astral realm, and he thought they were conquered. But it was not so. In the astral realm the law of oppos-ing forces has its dominion, but in the deeper realms of reality there are other laws.

In the elemental world a multitude of occult laws dominate, which are more like magic. Both translocation and transformation dominate this realm of materiality.

In the etheric, the law of Love dominates.

In the physical, the laws we know as mechanical laws are at work.

There are thus several levels that the Seeker needed to go through in order to transform the demons:

- First, the opposing forces in the astral realm (see Part I of this book).
- Secondly, the occult laws in the elemental world.
- Thirdly, Love in the etheric realm (see Part II).
- Finally, the total transformation of the physical layer of existence (see Part III).

This can also be described in another way, as everything in a sense happens in the elemental world – in successive layers or regions of the elemental world:

- First, in the third realm of the elemental world, a realm dominated by opposing forces.
- Secondly, in the second realm of the elemental world, where the dynamics of matter dominate.
- Thirdly, the first realm of the elemental world, where the deeper foundation of material existence is founded.

From another perspective I should emphasize that the etheric force nourishes and upholds all realms of the elemental world, as well as the etheric world itself, so that Love can thus transform beings or actions in all realms or worlds referred to.

Chapter 8

The Division of Thinking, Feeling and Will in the Spiritual Realm

As you will have seen from the first part of this book, access to experiencing earlier Earth epochs, as well as the fight against the demons, was helped by using shamanistic drugs such as ayahuasca and iboga. However, the Seeker was only partially freed through this method – actually, only from a third of his burden. Actually, he was only free in realtion to his astral body. Only his astral body was able to travel into the past in this way, and only through this astral body was he able to fight the demons of old.

In his conscious mind, in his 'I' and in his etheric body, he was still partially bound by the old demons and his old deeds.

The Seeker now understood that he had to go into the spiritual and elemental worlds in order to meet the remaining powers of the demons with his own spiritual forces. However, to enter the spiritual world, where neither time nor distance could hinder him from meeting and transforming the old demons, he had to be able to divide his thinking, feeling and will. According to Rudolf Steiner, that is the only conscious way to enter the spiritual world today – and to do this with your whole being, with the etheric body, the astral body and the 'I', you have to be able to do this consciously.

Throughout his early life, the Seeker had tended to be able to excarnate (to leave his body with his soul) – or, to put it another way, divide his thinking, feeling and will. However, this process had been involuntary, without his conscious effort. This ability may have been due to what he believed was epilepsy, or it may have been through what he thought were epileptic symptoms that appeared because of the described separation of the soul faculties (forces), obtained through karma and previous Earth lives.

Actually, the whole of humankind went through a spiritual evolution around 1899, when the previous strong link or binding between the thinking, feeling and will was loosened. Additionally, the gates to the third elemental realm opened, at least partly, in 1879. The second elemental realm followed in 1949 and the first elemental realm in 2019.

In a way, the whole of humanity passed the thresholds of the spiritual and elemental worlds in this way. The ancient Indian civilization knew this was going to happen at this present time, and described this as the ending of Kali Yuga, the Dark Age. The Dark Age was characterized by this tight binding of the three soul forces of thinking, feeling and the will. When this binding loosened, humanity would enter the Light Age, when access to the spiritual world would again become possible, but this time in full consciousness. According to ancient traditions, it was necessary to split human beings from the spiritual world so that in future we could find spirituality once again, but now in full freedom and consciousness. This consciousness is of utmost importance today, and this consciousness was awakened in the Seeker through the epileptic fits he experienced during his childhood.*

We have already seen how the Seeker attempted – and appeared to be successful in – fighting the demons. But, as already mentioned, it became apparent later that only some aspects of this karma had actually been resolved. More had to be done. In dealing with his karma relating to Atlantis and the total transformation of the demons, he had also to bring his etheric and conscious 'I' into this process, not only his astral body.

The mission was not yet accomplished. Karmic residues were still lingering throughout his spiritual body, and after some time he realized that he had to continue his quest.

In doing so, he also came to new realizations about the destruction of Atlantis, and how his relationship to the demons had to do with his urge to reincarnate in the new world that had emerged from the ruins of the Atlantean civilization.

As described above, the Seeker suffered from this 'disease' of the accidental division of his thinking, feeling and will, which he assumed was as a result of epilepsy. After having this condition for 32 years, however, it ended abruptly, in a matter of seconds. But the Seeker continued to use the 'techniques', that he had learned or developed through this 'condition', in order to enter into the spiritual world.

He described these techniques to me in the following way:

> The essential technique or tool to enter the spiritual world is
> to separate thinking, feeling and will, which are interlinked.
> Alternatively, we must separate the dimensions of the physical world as height, width, depth and time.

---

*This is described further in the book *Demons and Healing* (op. cit.).

As far as I know, the technique I describe is used in many different cultures,* although in different ways. Some cultures use meditation, chanting, postures, sexuality and shamanic rituals, whilst some choose to use psychotropic plants, toad- or frog toxins, or combinations of several of these elements.

As feeling is related to depth, the easiest and best way is to start by separating depth from width and height. This is done by a kind of daydreaming, as when you merge or wander from the wide expanses of your surroundings. Many experience this state of mind during, for example, a boring lecture or conversation, when you suddenly fade away and do not really hear what is being said. To enter the spiritual world, we must develop this art of 'fading away'. Then, thinking and will are left behind and we just float in the cosmos. Then we lose our everyday ability to be intelligent, calculating, or to plan or think logically. We do not think as 'intelligently' as before, and we are unable to 'will' anything. We feel a slight change in our hearing, similar to tinnitus, and the colours of the landscape change a little – a slight turning towards violet.

After an additional 32 years of practising and understanding the division described above, a deeper realization now entered the Seeker's mind. He had understood more deeply that the whole cosmos is actually the inverted body of one's own self, or the collective human organism. The complete skull is the whole of the cosmos, inverted. The complete body is the whole cosmos, inverted.

One morning the Seeker experienced the dividing of his thinking, feeling and will – but not in his senses, not in his present-day body or consciousness, but deep inside his skull, in the region where his head turned into the whole cosmos. He experienced the ability to enter the spiritual world – not in the present world of human bodies, but deep within the cosmos itself, deep within his own head.

The three divine forces of the cosmos then became accessible to him: the three fundamental forces of the cosmos which make up the

---

*In academic terms, this change between the non-separation and the separation of the soul abilities is called a 'noetic slippage'. This slippage is described as a spiritual state where the mind changes between chaos and order, between light and darkness, between the Dionysian and the Apollonian, between the noetic and the chthonic.

whole of everything, which make up all the physical laws, and which even explain gravity as a function of the cosmic will.

These three forces can be found in all aspects of cosmic life, human life and philosophy. One of the clearest expressions of these three forces is found in 'The Lord's Prayer'.

The Seeker tried to explain this aspect of 'The Lord's Prayer' to me when I visited him one day.

> You have to understand that feeling, thinking and will are the foundation of all that is created. They are free cosmic forces, expressing the Father God, the Son Christ and the Holy Spirit, as well as the Mother God, the Sacred Daughter and the Holy Soul. It is only when these three forces get intertwined, when they become bound to each other, that the material universe can and does appear. This was the real 'big bang', which actually was not a bang at all.
>
> If you are then able to separate these three forces, if you can free them from each other, then you can enter the spiritual world; then you *are in* the spiritual world. The three are in everything. When the three become free, then they become the one – the one freedom or the one God.

He continued:

> You see, my friend, here in our earthly form we have the three forces bound together in one body. That is why we are here. When we are able to separate these three forces, then we can enter the spiritual world.
>
> These three forces can be seen everywhere in the revelations brought to us from the spiritual world.
>
> Let us consider 'The Lord's Prayer'. This prayer shows us where we came from, from what forces we were created. Furthermore, it shows us how we should deal with these three forces in this physical world. If we manage to separate these forces without getting trapped within karma, we may once again enter the spiritual world.
>
> Our Father, who art in heaven,
> hallowed be thy name,
> thy kingdom come,

thy will be done,
on earth as it is in heaven.

Give us this day our daily bread.
And forgive us our trespasses,
as we forgive those
who trespass against us.

And lead us not into temptation,
but deliver us from evil.

For thine is the kingdom,
and the power, and the glory,
for ever and ever.

    Amen.

First, we address the three great forces of the spiritual world:

> 1. Name, resembling the thinking.
> 2. Kingdom, resembling the feeling.
> 3. Will, resembling the will.

Then we ask for these three forces to reign *on the earth* as they do in the heavens. On this earth we are seduced by and act against the three cosmic forces with:

> 1. Bread, resembling the will.
> 2. Trespasses, resembling the thinking.
> 3. Temptation, resembling the feeling.

Then again, we have the hailing of the three cosmic forces as they will appear to us if we are able to conquer our earthly sins against the cosmic laws:

> 1. Kingdom, resembling the feeling.
> 2. Power, resembling the will.
> 3. Glory, resembling the thinking.

I hesitated, as I did not understand what my old friend the Seeker was trying to describe to me. He saw my hesitation and began again to explain:

All forces in the world can be divided into three fundamental forces; three forces that are the foundation of all other forces – the foundation of what is even called dark matter. For example, gravity is just an expression of cosmic willpower. These forces are of a spiritual nature and our material eyes and senses only see the material expression of them.

Now, when we want to divide these three forces in our physical world, or more to the point become aware that they are already somewhat divided and can easily be further divided, we have to become acquainted with the separate potentials of each force. There are, to my limited knowledge, two ways to do this, but there are probably more.

The first thing we have to do in each of these ways is to strengthen the separate forces and abilities of thinking, feeling and will. Then we can, by way of mental 'gliding', separate the feeling from the thinking.

We can trace old knowledge about the three cosmic forces in almost every part of the *Bible* – in fact, in every part of reality itself, if only we look for it. Let us for a moment consider the beginning of the Gospel of St John:

In the beginning was the Word, and the Word was with God, and the Word was God. He was with God in the beginning. Through him all things were made; without him nothing was made that has been made. In him was life, and that life was the light of all mankind. The light shines in the darkness, and the darkness has not overcome it. There was a man sent from God whose name was John. He came as a witness to testify concerning that light, so that through him all might believe. He himself was not the light; he came only as a witness to the light. The true light that gives light to everyone was coming into the world. He was in the world, and though the world was made through him, the world did not recognize him. He came to that which was his own, but his own did not receive him. Yet to all who did receive him, to those who believed in his name, he gave the right to become children of God—children born not of natural descent, nor of human decision or a husband's

will, but born of God. The Word became flesh and made his dwell-
ing among us. We have seen his glory, the glory of the one and only
Son, who came from the Father, full of grace and truth.

Here again we can see this mysterious threefold repetition
relating to *thinking, feeling* and *the will*. In the first verse it is
stated that:

1) 'In the beginning *was* the Word...' Here we encounter
the being or existence of the Word – it *was*. This is pure existence, as in *thinking*.

2) '... and the Word was *with God*...' Here we get the
impression of a relationship between the Word and God, a
feeling relationship between them, as in *feeling*.

3) '... and the Word *was God*...' Here we get the impression that the word was in action, it was God, it acted as God,
as in *the will*.

We encounter the same cosmic forces concerning the
being of the Word in verses 2 and 3, although here it is a
little more hidden. Then, in verses 4 and 5, we clearly see the
same, relating to the essence of the Word.

1) 'In him was life' (the existence of life, the pure life, as
in *thinking*).

2) '... And that life was the light of all mankind' (the feeling of the life, as in *feeling*)

3) '... And the light shineth in darkness; and the darkness
comprehended it not.' Here we feel the action of the life, as
in *the will*.

The Seeker paused here for a moment and became thoughtful. Then he
continued:

There are deep secrets hidden in the construction of both
the Lord's Prayer and in the Gospels, secrets that I cannot
fully comprehend. One of these is the succession or place
where thinking, feeling and will is mentioned in the three
'sections' of the Lord's Prayer. In the first part, of original
heavenly order, thinking is mentioned first, which resembles
the third hierarchy of divine spiritual beings. Then feeling,

which resembles the second hierarchy, and lastly the will, which resembles the first hierarchy. This is the order when we look up at the spiritual world. Here on the Earth, where these hierarchies and forces are materialized, the will is mentioned first, then thinking and finally feeling. This is the earthly order. When we have managed to transform these forces, they will become divine again, but then in the image of human abilities, making feeling the first force, then the will and lastly thinking. These three orders or successions of the divine forces tell very much about the whole cosmogenesis, the total evolution of man.

The Seeker kept silent for a while, deep in thought. I recalled what he had written in a book he had published on pulse-diagnosis. I found the book standing on his shelf, and read the relevant passage out loud to him:

> Rudolf Steiner said that the entanglement of thinking, feeling and the will, which are three cosmic and divine forces originating in the spiritual world and not within ourselves, is the main reason why we are anchored in this physical world.
>
> I will explain this in more detail, as this is of crucial importance to both myself and the readers of this book, especially relating to describing and seeing demons.
>
> When man, consisting of body, soul and spirit, incarnates in the physical world, our feeling, thinking and will are intertangled, intertwined, connected and bound together. The real content, function, power and origin of the three soul faculties (thinking, feeling and will) are hidden from us because they overshadow each other. Modern science would have us believe that thinking, feeling and will are just faculties developed or produced by ourselves, and forever interdependent. This is a serious mistake that keeps us in ignorance, in *maya*. This is what Morpheus and Neo in the film *The Matrix* call 'the Matrix'. It is what we may call the 'greater illusion'.*

---

*The 'lesser illusion' is within the spiritual world itself, when souls abiding there are lost or stuck in the belief that there is no way out, no way to reincarnate, no love and no Christ.

It is as if we would believe that the colours that we see are within the eye, created by ourselves, and that the sounds that we hear are within the ear, created by the brain. It is the same with thinking, feeling and will. These are three cosmic forces which we may use as our own and as such become part of the cosmos, become part of the divine, part of the spirit world.

We can work wonders, even deeds that some people would call magic, if we can separate, i.e. liberate or set free from one another, our three soul faculties/powers (thinking, feeling and/or will).

Will is the strongest but most hidden power. Feeling is the half-conscious and half-hidden power. Thinking is the least hidden power.

The Seeker remained quiet as I read to him from his book.

'Yes', he said, 'it is so'. He explained further:

But there are two, maybe even three different ways, or I must rather say 'places', where we may divide the think-ing, feeling and will. And this insight is new to me, as it is to you, my friend. And this new insight also tells me that I have to face my three great demons again. What I did last time was not enough.

The three forces may be separated here in this world, or they may be separated in the spiritual world itself. To say it in a more detailed way, they may be divided in the astral world, in the etheric world and in the physical world. The material world, which we usually think of as 'our' world, is for me at the present time too mysterious to comprehend, but maybe this is the fourth place or level where the dividing may take place.

I may enter the spiritual world by dividing the three soul forces, but I may also enter the spiritual world through turn-ing my whole self inside-out, as what happens when you pull off a surgical glove. Then your whole body becomes the outside, becomes the totality of the cosmos. You become the cosmos, and in this situation you understand that the whole of the cosmos is the human being – the entire human being.

In a way, then, the dividing will have eight possibilities: four here and four there.

In this situation, it is also possible to divide thinking, feeling and will, and in this way you enter into the totality of cosmic forces and not only your own cosmic/human forces.

In this way, you can also enter the cosmos much more deeply, and consequently you are able consciously to meet your demons in the totality of your being, with the etheric body, the astral body and the 'I'.

This way of entering the cosmic forces happened to me not long ago – and when I had entered the cosmos thus, I understood that I still had to deal with the demons.

He paused for a moment then went on:

This understanding did not come to me until I found the ruby.

Chapter 9

Finding the Ruby. Opening the Second Veil of the Cosmos. The Second Elemental Realm

The physical thread or lead to solving the remaining karma and understanding the destruction of Atlantis – along with the Seeker´s part in this terrible catastrophe – was initiated by the finding of the ruby.

Let us remind ourselves what C. said to the Seeker in Part I:

> You stabbed me with a huge dagger, ornamented with a big ruby on the shaft. I loved you so much and you killed me. I have had problems excusing you for that. It was not necessary at all. We could have solved that problem; it was, after all, done to protect you from yourself.

*

Some years later, in January 2017, the Seeker felt that he had to go to India. Together with his wife, he travelled from Oslo to Abu Dhabi, where they had a stopover for two days. During that stay, they went out into the desert and experienced the desolation of the wilderness. The Seeker stood for a while by himself and looked out into the wide expanses of the Arabian desert. A movement in the distance caught his attention, and he looked more carefully. There he saw a group of jinns, or 'demons of the desert', as described in *One Thousand and One Nights*.

The jinns looked very different from all the other elementary beings he had seen previously. The Norwegian elemental beings of the third realm of the elemental world, such as nisser and dverger and even trolls, looked like nice schoolboys in relation to the jinns. The jinns looked fierce; they had long teeth, sharp like a tiger´s canines, and they had a very bloodthirsty look in their blood-shot eyes. The Seeker felt a certain fear as he watched them. Then one of the jinns, possibly their leader, caught sight of him as he was studying them. The jinn *saw* that he *saw* them, and the whole group turned to the Seeker, rushing towards him.

The leader of the jinns stopped just in front of the Seeker and pierced him with his fierce eyes. He tried to 'enter' the Seeker (to possess him), and the Seeker – who was used to elemental beings and keeping them at a distance – had difficulties in keeping the jinn away. The strength of the jinn was remarkable. He pressed on towards the Seeker, and tried to get into his soul. Then the Seeker made the sign of Michael, as taught by Rudolf Steiner, and in a second the jinn was unable to fight. The whole group turned away and rushed further back into the desert.

The sign of Michael

Later that day, when the Seeker had arrived back at the hotel, he asked some local Arabs about the jinn. Many of them had seen these creatures, and they were amazed that a white foreigner, a Christian even, had been able to see them. They had no sensible information about them, however.

The Seeker and his wife continued their travels to Chennai in India.

When walking past a jeweller's shop, the Seeker had a strong intuition that he should enter. It was as if someone or something shouted his name and asked him to enter inside. In the shop he asked to see the rubies they had, and the owner of the shop brought forth a collection of the precious stones.

One of the rubies almost cried out to him; it looked different from all the others, at least to his eyes. He picked the ruby up between his fingers and looked deep inside it. Inside the red stone he could see a white hexagonal structure. This structure looked like the cell of a bee hive. From each of its hexagonal corners there was what appeared to be a spider web, projecting out into space. He sank into the process of observation, and the spider web projected itself into his head, causing his crown chakra to start to move. It moved in the same way that his heart chakra had started to move several years ago, when he had first made a breakthrough in his work. Now, both his heart and his crown chakra moved.

He bought the ruby and carried it on his person whilst travelling in India. He often took it up, sinking into the web-like structure. It was like entering further and deeper into the spiritual or elemental world, more than he had ever done before.

When they came to Kerala, on the west coast of India, he found a jeweller that was able to place the ruby in the setting of a golden ring, and after that he wore the ruby on his finger all the time.

Some weeks later, he understood the importance of this ruby, although he had no idea of its value when he had bought it. The finding of the ruby felt to him like when the farmer in Ireland offered him the land where 'his' pyramid had once been standing. The ruby wanted to come back to its owner.

A few days later he got a message from C. She felt that something had happened. Something was happening to her karma. He told her that he had found and bought a ruby that had called to him, and she immediately felt that it was the very ruby that had ornamented the dagger with which he had killed her, some 4,000 years ago. She wept.

Some days later, he woke up in the morning feeling that something had changed. He lay there in his bed quietly and realized that he was actually in the spiritual world. He could experience the three powers of thinking, feeling and will and could easily divide them within the spiritual world itself. Before, he had been able to divide the three forces within himself, within this physical world, and through such means had been able to enter the spiritual/elemental world – but now he could divide the forces *in the spiritual world*, or rather, while they were still cosmic forces. He had obtained freedom within freedom.

He didn't doubt for a moment that this had to do with the crown chakra. The heart chakra had been necessary in the process of dividing the forces within himself, as the heart was within him. However, inside the cranium, where he was already in the vast cosmos, he could now also divide. He was already stretched out like a glove, so in a way he did not divide the forces outside of himself but *inside* himself, i.e. when he was already in this cosmic self.

Chapter 10

Revisiting Ireland. The Deeper and Cosmic Dimensions of the Demons

As the reader may remember from Part I, the Seeker's access to the past was not fully apparent until he had travelled to Ireland and visited the old mystery places where he had once committed his dark deeds.

He had now twice visited these ancient areas of Ireland. The first time he had been lifted up into the spiritual world in a total division of his thinking, feeling and will. The second time, 22 years later, he had been able to free himself from the astral grip of the demons.

Now, on a third visit, he knew he had to penetrate into the deeper areas of the cosmos in full consciousness, and there to divide his soul forces. Then, once free from all earthly burdens, he knew he should change and transform the elemental/etheric aspect of the demons that had been his 'companions' for so long.

He travelled to Ireland in the spring of 2017. At the airport he hired a car as always, and travelled southwest. He intended to visit Roscrea before Langford and Sligo, the opposite direction of travel to his last visit. The last time he had begun with the *thinking*, then the *feeling* and lastly *the will*. This time he wanted to start with the will at Roscrea, continue with the feeling and then end up with the thinking. For a moment he contemplated his Irish mission that had now occurred three times – three repetitions of the changing order of thinking, feeling and will, as in the Lord's Prayer.

Was he praying this prayer through his Irish quest?

He arrived at Roscrea in the late afternoon, a bright and warm spring day. He found a guesthouse in the outskirts of the town, very close to the Roscrea Golf Club, situated close to the Ballaghmore Bog (a nature reserve). After settling in his room and drinking 'a jolly good cup of tea', he took a walk in the surroundings. He entered into the bog area, where four small lakes were to be found. There were three small lakes on one side of the railway line, and the fourth on the other side. A small river, the Bunnow, had its starting point or source in the bog. This area was new to him. He had not come across it the last time he visited this part of Ireland in 2015.

He sat down at the shore of the largest lake within the bog area and rested. It was now close to sunset and all life in the surrounding nature had started to calm down. The birds sang less and the insects had become quieter.

Suddenly a small leprechaun showed up. He recognized the little creature from his first visit to Ireland. As previously, the creature looked like a small man and was shaped as such, but the Seeker knew he was not human. The Seeker greeted him – leprechauns are usually perceived as 'male', although that might be an illusion – in a friendly manner. The leprechaun returned his friendly gaze. The leprechaun's behaviour this time was quite different to the previous time, however. Then, there had been two leprechauns and they did not utter a word, did not smile, but only pointed to the direction in which they wanted the Seeker to travel. This time the leprechaun smiled, and after some moments he actually started to speak. (Was this again caused by the development from imagination to inspiration and to intuition?)

He said something like what is expressed below, although not of course in the same words:

> Last time we met you did not even know the way. We had to point it out to you. Later, we followed you without you knowing. We worked through your soul so that you were able to take up the fight with the demons that were connected to you. You were able to fight them on the level of your feelings, your emotions, and as such you freed yourself from them. But there are deeper realms of existence in which you are still bound. In these deeper realms we find the connection to the future, to your next life on this Earth... and to the past. To reach these layers, you have to penetrate deeper into the spiritual/elemental world, to the depths that are hidden by two and three veils respectively (to the second and first realm of the elemental world, maybe even to the etheric world). To reach this, you have to understand that *you are* the cosmos itself, that you are actually identical to that vast cosmos. *That cosmos is you.* Also, you have to understand that both the cosmos and yourself are threefold, are intertwined in three forces, thinking, feeling and will. This you have now understood.
>
> Now you are ready to penetrate into the etheric depths of existence – yes, even into the physical realms of existence, hidden behind the three veils. Here you will meet the demons again, in their etheric and karmic projections, although it is

possible that you are still not ready for the meeting of your karma and your demonic tendencies in the physical realm. If that is the case, then this must be done later.

The Seeker did not understand this last sentence, the consequences of which we will see in the unravelling of his demonic karma in Part III of this book.

The leprechaun ended with the warning: 'Be ready for this now. It will happen very soon…!'

After this monologue, the leprechaun gazed at the Seeker for a long time, as if to be sure that he had understood the meaning of what he had said. The Seeker made an imagination in his head in order to picture the meaning, and the leprechaun seemed to understand the picture he presented and appeared to be content. Then the leprechaun slowly faded away, dissolving into the landscape from whence he had come.

In the late evening, after the meeting with the leprechaun, the Seeker felt very tired. He thought about what he had to do… and what it would be like to meet the demons again. The last time he had met them was in the astral realm, a realm where vivid illusions or hallucinations may prevail. But now he had to face them in the etheric and spiritual/elemental realm. How would that be? How could that be done? How could he prepare?

As night drew near, the Seeker fell into a deep sleep.

He had a vivid dream.

He dreamt that he was in a vast forest. The trees were alien to him. The forms of the branches were like ornaments, the stems twirled like corkscrews; the whole forest was living and moving and then, after a while, talking in a strange and unintelligible language. He went deeper and deeper into the forest, and came to what he thought might be the middle. There he found a glade, a circular area without trees. The grass here was shining in an unusual bright and green colour, and millions of small flowers grew everywhere. In the middle of the glade he saw a fair, young woman sitting in the grass stroking the head of a sleeping man who lay in her lap. She had her head bent down over his head. He went closer and saw that the man was not sleeping. He was dead. The young woman looked up with tears in her eyes and sank into the gaze of the Seeker. Slowly he went closer, looking at the dead man all the time. Blood was gently seeping from his side, into the grass and flowers. The Seeker stretched out his arm and touched the blood with a finger. He took his finger up to his mouth and touched his tongue. The blood tasted bitter.

Immediately he understood the voices of the forest, which until now he had not been able to comprehend. He now deciphered words and understood the language of the trees. He looked around and watched the trees. Suddenly he could see their faces, their bodies, their eyes… He could understand their language… He could even communicate with them.

Then he woke up. Now he felt ready to face the demons. This was the time that he intended fully to meet the old demons again.

He spent the day without any purpose or activity, mainly in the room of his guesthouse. As evening approached and the final encounter with his three demons grew closer, he went back to the lake where he had been the previous day. He arrived at the shore and sat down.

Sitting there in the late afternoon, he started to feel a kind of tingling in his ears, similar to that of tinnitus. The surroundings grew slightly darker, although there were no clouds in the sky and the night had not yet come. A faint smell filled the air, and a very quiet crackling sound like broken glass. He felt some movements to the right of his vision, and inside his head he heard a voice saying, 'Look at us!'

He looked around closely and could see the faces of the trees, of the plants and bushes. They were talking to him; not in words, but in meanings, in concepts.

This had happened to him before, between the ages of 5 and 12 years; but this talking with trees and plants had faded to almost nothing in his teens. Later in life, his communications with the spiritual world had been taken up with pathogenic structures, demons and diseases.* During the last five years, the realm of pure and beneficial life forces, of the good and light side of the universe, had started to reveal itself to him again.

He thought about the three hierarchies of angels revealing themselves in the Lord's Prayer, mirroring also in the three elemental realms making up the material world.

Long-forgotten exchanges with the world of trees emerged in his soul. It was as if he was meeting an old love again. The deep wisdom-filled knowledge of the trees arose like light in his consciousness. He felt an intense joy, and in this joy he saw the image of the leprechaun. The leprechaun was smiling again, smiling from ear to ear, as if his mission was complete.

---

*See my book *Demons and Healing* (op. cit.).

The trees told him how he could conquer the three demons, both in the etheric, the elemental and in the spiritual dimensions. If he was able to conquer them in the elemental realm, then almost immediately they would also be beaten in the etheric realm, and could then be transformed into the light from whence they had come and to where they truly belonged.

So, conquer was not the right word, and he had to change what he had thought earlier – change his attitude towards the demons. The merging in the elemental realm with the nature beings had changed his mind from 'fighting' – which was a common feeling in the astral realm – to transforming, which characterized the elemental/etheric realm, just as all plants and trees continuously transform their life forms, their leaves, seeds and their appearance. All of these are trans-formations of earlier forms. Even if some of those earlier forms were poisonous, the later forms could still be beneficial. The same applied to the long-feared demons; they could also be transformed into good forces – into the good and light elementals which they had once been.

The Seeker sat there at the lake until it was almost dark. He watched the small floating islands there, made of turf. He watched the birds and the insects. He watched the whole of nature. He watched the whole cosmos.

He understood what he had to do. He had to meet his demons in all realms of the elemental and etheric worlds, maybe even in the illusory reflection of the elemental world, which is called the physical/mate-rial world – not only in the astral world, as he had last time.

Was he prepared for this? If not, how should or could he prepare? The nature beings had not given him any hint of how he should get ready for the encounter with his demons.

He started to reason, to consider his possibilities. The last time he fought the demons, he had the help of the nature beings and the sha-man. The powers of the shaman and the shamanistic herbs are nature powers, from below. This time he had to turn to help from above. Yes, that was the solution. At the very end of his last battle with the demons, for a moment he had turned to Christ, and that gave him the ultimate strength to pursue the victory.

He remembered his demonic fight in his *astral* body. He had known he had to go *through* the demons and to get to the other side, where he knew 'the light' was waiting for him. The people that trusted him had been waiting – the end of the long, long path of evil. When the victory was won, they had hailed him. Yet still he had not seen or come to know how he had hurt his people, how he had closed the hearts of the ones that were dependent on him. He had known there was still more to do...

So, this is how he had to fight in the spiritual realms. He had to trust; trust the angels, the archangels... and the Saviour... the Christ.

This fight had to be in the spirit of the Christ, which means not really 'a fight' or 'a victory' over the demons, but a *transformation* of them – a changing through love. This would also lead to a change in the hearts of the ones he had once let down so badly.

The night approached rapidly. There was still a faint light, and the silhouettes of the trees growing around the little lake became more accentuated. The wind held its breath. All was quiet, with only the night insects allowing their sounds to be heard.

Around midnight the three demons appeared. At first, he did not understand their presence; he just felt a certain dizziness. It was as if he had entered some alien realm of reality. The light from the stars changed somewhat in intensity, the faint sound of the night insects became sharper, the smell of nature more intense. He tilted his head a little towards the right and observed that the surroundings started to move, to shiver, like small ripples in a summer breeze. He had entered another realm – the elemental realm – and another reality.

The demons were totally different this time, not so fierce and frightening. They were not filled with anger or passion, as they were in his last encounter. They appeared to be filled more with streaming currents, like blood circulation, as when a drop of ink falls into water, like an etheric octopus or jellyfish.

In a way, this new encounter was more frightening to the Seeker than his previous experience. Last time it was all so much more 'real'. This time it felt like the demons could avoid his attempt to fight them, to transform them. They were conquered in the astral realm, but still active in the etheric and the elemental realms. And the last victory had made them more conscious, more careful. They knew his strength... and they were cautious.

The Seeker sat silent and motionless for a while – just watching, just waiting... He knew that the only strength demons actually have is what is taken from their opponents, their enemies, their victims... Thus, in this case, from the Seeker himself. Therefore, as long as he sat there motionless, the demons could do nothing. He could sit there the whole night and just watch, think, observe... until he had found their weak spot, their point of transformation.

And so he sat there the whole night, motionless, observing how the 'arms' of the demons moved, how dense they were, how strong they might be, contemplating how he was supposed to transform them. Fighting them, as he had done in the astral realm, would not work here.

Towards the morning he had achieved a deeper understanding of the demons. They seemed to have two parts, two distinct areas within their energetic structure. It was as if the upper part had a different movement, a different rhythm or vibration, than the lower part. The upper part rotated against the sun whilst the lower part rotated with the sun. The colours of the two parts were also somewhat different. The upper part had some deep but faint colouring to it, as in the colours found inside a mussel's shell. The colours of mother-of-pearl can only be seen inside the shell if you stand at a right angle to it, as well as to the incoming light. The colours of the upper part of the demons could only be seen if he mentally 'stood' at a right angle to the moving structure, the moving demonic structure. The Seeker could not see any colours in the lower part, even though he tried in every possible way... Then he became interested in the space between the two parts. The space between!

He had become aware of this 'space between' phenomenon many years ago, during his third visit to the stone circle of Stonehenge. In Part I of this book we saw how the Seeker, standing before the huge stones, perceived far distant epochs and places – as like a transparent film – flickering *between* the stones. Likewise, he now perceived between the structures an area of neutrality, where the forces of the upper and lower parts of the demons could be transformed.

He had worked with the same 'problem' in his therapeutic work for twenty years. Eventually he realized that in ordinary or normal treatment of disease – whether you treat the symptoms or the cause – the pathological structure in most instances is only translocated to other parts of the body or even to other individuals or animals.* According to anthroposophy, these demons are born as a result of human misdeeds and thoughts, created both in the present and the past. The life force of the demons is sustained by the geopathic radiation of the Earth, which in reality is an energetic expression of our karma. Ultimately, they seek the experience of the material world by attaching to both man and animals.

---

*See further in *Spiritual Translocation* (Temple Lodge Publishing, 2020).

The first hint as to how to transform these demons of pathological structure came to him from Judith von Halle,[*] a writer and mystic living in Berlin. She had said that to avoid translocation of the disease, one should treat with a 'Christ-consciousness', based on principles of universal love.

During the crucifixion, Christ hung in the middle, between two robbers; one representing luciferic crimes, the other ahrimanic crimes.

- The ahrimanic criminal mocked Jesus Christ (and is condemned for eternity to the Eighth Sphere).
- The luciferic criminal begged to join Christ when he came to his kingdom (and Jesus Christ, who has even promised Lucifer access to the heavens one day, granted the criminal his wish).

Going through all these thoughts, gathering his experiences from both Stonehenge and his medical work, the realization dawned upon the Seeker that approaching the middle part of the demons, and embracing them in love, held the possibility of transforming them in both their elemental, etheric and physical aspects. It was certainly worth a try.

Now the dawn had started to emerge. The shimmering of the light over the eastern horizon became stronger and stronger, bringing the Seeker back to the everyday world. Chirping birds started to offer their song to the cosmos. The day was arriving.

He felt a strong sense of joy with the rising of the sun, and he also felt strong. However, tired after the night of watching and waiting, he decided to sleep during the day and to meet the demons again at nightfall. He then went back to his guesthouse, ate some food and went to bed.

---

[*]Judith von Halle was born in Berlin in 1972 and is an architect by profession. During Easter 2004 the stigmata of Christ appeared on her. Since that occurrence, she has only been able to consume water – that is, no solid nourishment. She now gives lectures and writes books. In the first part of her book *And If He Has Not Been Raised...* she describes her experience, as well as the irreversible and substantial changes in her bodily constitution during and since receiving the stigmata. This book should be considered as the basis for her subsequent publications. Her lectures and books are mostly but not exclusively concerned with Christology, whereby she adheres to Rudolf Steiner's work on the same subject. As is true with other cases of stigmata, Judith von Halle can 'see' the events that took place during the life of Jesus Christ.

Almost immediately, he fell asleep, but his sleep was not deep. He woke up several times, and each time the same dream appeared strongly in his mind. It went like this:

He was surrounded by the living world. He looked around and rejoiced over all the beautiful colours, all the pleasant smells of nature, the clouds in the sky and the distant mountains. He heard the gentle noises of a nearby creek and the birds were singing all around. All was well... but something disturbed his mind. There was a part of him that did not belong here, a part of him that belonged somewhere else. He faced a riddle, and this riddle took the form of approaching darkness. He looked at the darkness and in the centre of it he could see, faintly, a light. As the darkness grew stronger, the light at its centre also grew stronger. He looked intensively at this light, which started to take form. He could see movements in the light. The movements resembled the movements of the demons he had encountered the night before. One thing was changed, however. The small middle area of the demons was now more open, and in this part a strong light started to shine. The light came from a being that looked like a knight, an old-fashioned medieval knight with metal-plated armour and a shining sword. Lying in front of his feet were three fierce animals: a dog, an ox and a snake. The knight lifted his head and looked straight at the Seeker, speaking in a low voice: 'You must conquer the three animals within your own heart. Then my sword and my light will be yours. Then you can transform the upper and the lower parts of the demons.'

The knight pointed to a vast field in front of him, just behind the three animals. It was a field that included many plants that humans use for food: carrots, potatoes, cabbage and more. The plants needed something. They did not thrive, and they cried for help. Then the gardener's daughter came with seven cans of water.

The Seeker thought about the words of the knight each time he woke up, and by early evening he believed he had understood the message and its instructions.

Chapter 11

Meeting the Old Demons Again

The next evening the Seeker once again wandered from his lodgings towards the marshy area with the four small lakes. He took a longer route this time as he wanted to come from a different direction. He went around Ballaghmore Bog and then followed the Bunnow River up to the centre of the bog. Here he went directly towards the shore of the little lake where he had sat the previous night and studied the energetic anatomy of the demons. It was here that he had discovered their weak point, the middle, where the Christ-force may be found.

He now planned to meet the demons from his own heart centre and to direct all his power of warmth and love towards their middle part, where he assumed they probably had something that resembled a heart-like structure, before it had been destroyed by his own actions 40,000 years ago... or longer.

He arrived at the shore of the little lake and sat down. Now all he had to do was wait. Again, he immersed his soul in the falling dusk, just as he had the previous evening. This immersing oneself in the sounds and the colours of the fading day gives much strength to the soul. He listened to the buzzing of insects, the fading song of birds preparing for night, and he watched the slowly fading light bringing forth the emerging silhouettes of the trees.

Then the same thing happened as on the previous evening. He slipped out of everyday reality. His feeling, thinking and will separated and, in a sense, became defenceless. When they are together they support each other, 'looking after' each other. When they are alone and by themselves, they seem to lose some of their bearing. In that case, the only force that can direct them is the consciousness of the human being.

When the feeling, thinking and will are separated, all perception changes. The remaining colours, the silhouettes, the buzzing of the insects and the fading tones of the birds all changed, becoming more intense and sharper. Then the demons appeared.

Although he knew he was prepared, he felt a certain fear. This fear was not the same as when he had faced the demons in the astral element. No, this fear was completely different. The astral fright was pure fear; fear of being hurt or attacked. It was the old fear of being sucked into the power of the dark path, the power of black magic – the same path he had been lured to follow so long ago; maybe as long as 40,000 years ago.

He still felt the urge to power in his blood. But this new fear had filled his mind. He knew the power that these demons possessed. He knew that they possessed power over the elemental realms. In his work as a healer, as an acupuncturist and as a veterinarian, he could use these powers to heal. He would heal in this way for the benefit of his patients, with a deep wish to do good. From him, these powers would find a way to penetrate all his patients – to heal – *yes… but…* and this he now saw very clearly… If, when directed to the patient he was treating, the healing energy was not immersed with love and the power of Christ-consciousness, it would in fact be bound or linked to the dark forces.

In his life he had seen and experienced several healers, acupuncturists or other therapists working in different areas of healing. They were all doing good work; they were healing their patients and those patients were happy with the treatments and satisfied with how they had changed… usually for the better.

But was it so? Apart from the fact that the disease could only be translocated to another living entity, the etheric energy used in the act of treatment could also be tinted or 'stolen' by other forces, independent of whether the disease was simply translocated or even transformed.

The Seeker had looked deeply into these matters many times. He had studied therapists that had received their training from so-called 'dark brotherhoods'. These groups of people, through many lives trained in mastering magic, teach different ways of healing to students and adepts, whilst the students themselves believe they attain ordinary medical training from ordinary schools or institutes. The ways of healing taught in these schools might appear good and efficient, really helping patients, but there is a 'catch'. The healing is not *direct*. The dark brotherhoods have created a sort of *middle chamber* within the healing process. And in this chamber, there are three spiritual doors: one door leading in, one door leading out (which is the 'real' healing), and then a third door through which the masters of the dark brotherhoods can take their part of the healing energy. They may then use this energy as they wish, often in destructive ways, and usually to gain more power for themselves.

The therapist will then become bound to these dark brotherhoods for a long time, especially after death. The Seeker had seen, with his own spiritual eyes, how several groups or 'institutions' had practised this form of black magic. For example, these dark lords have gained access within specific cults related to Odin – either with or without the knowledge of the founders of the groups or organizations in question. The Seeker had experienced or observed that some Reiki healers were trapped after death; trapped in order to serve the dark brotherhoods. These brotherhoods had even managed to get their ugly fingers inside some homeopathic practices, for example in the potentization of the 'LM' remedies.* They always create this fissure, this extra door, this hole, through which they 'tap out' their power (often about 10% of the energy, just as the Church did in medieval times).

If the Seeker continued to be connected to the demons, he would be their servant for all eternity. If he did not resist them now, if he did not find the strength to break free in both the etheric and the physical realms of existence, they would own him.

This process of breaking loose was also a renunciation of power, for he had to become totally free of the desire to have power or control.

He had thought that if he were able to break free within the astral realm – where the feelings were, where the emotions were – then he would become completely free. However, he had discovered that it is not so; we have to be free in all levels of existence, even in the material realm. Of course, this will take a very long time, and we have to work on the spiritualization of all layers or realms of our being:

- The astral body has to be transformed to Manas.
- The etheric body has to be transformed to Buddhi.
- The physical body has to be transformed to Atma, which is the final step on the way to liberation.**

These thoughts flashed through his mind as he encountered the demons. As he watched them, he felt that this time they expected something from him. In a flash of realization, the Seeker understood that they believed he was still interested in etheric power, as he now worked as a healer. They thought they could tempt him with the power of healing, making him believe that they would turn him into a renowned and famous healer. But what the demons did not

---

*The LM or quintamillesimal scale in homeopathy dilutes the drug to one part in 50,000 parts of dilutent.

**These are teachings of Rudolf Steiner. See his *Occult Science, An Outline* (Rudolf Steiner Press).

understand was that he had already seen through this illusion. To treat only from oneself leads to a translocation of disease. He had understood that the only true healing comes from the *middle point*, from the Christ energy, from the Christ consciousness, and not from his own forces and strength. 'Not I, but Christ in me', as Paul (St Paul) had said.

One of the demons now said: 'We will work with you and make you a better healer.'

'I will only heal through Christ from now on', he replied.

'You will be famous, and can do much good', two of the demons exclaimed, speaking in unison.

'I am not interested in that, I will only heal as long as the cosmic energies, not myself, are valued and worshipped', he replied. The three demons were in confusion. Then they tried a third attack, saying:

'Then you will be rich.' This was the easiest temptation to withstand, thought the Seeker, answering:

'I do not care about money.'

He remembered an incident when he had euthanized four kittens just after he had graduated as a veterinarian. A famous troubadour had made an appointment, and he wanted to put down the kittens as he and his guitar were going on a tour around the whole of Norway. Flattered by the appearance of this famous Norwegian celebrity at his veterinary practice, the Seeker granted his request to kill the four healthy, new-born kittens. He still remembered the act of injecting their abdomens with a substance that would induce their deadly sleep. He normally charged 10 Norwegian kroner per murdered kitten, and after the deed was done he asked the celebrity to pay 40 kroner. As soon as he had uttered these words, something happened to or within his consciousness. It was at that point that he realized what he had done at a spiritual level. The whole reality changed, and with wide open eyes he watched as his small office became dark and stretched out into a tunnel. From the tunnel he heard his own voice echoing back the cost of the murder; but instead of 40 kroner, the price became 30 silver coins.

The significance of this amount is of course that it was the same price that Judas received when he betrayed Christ. Unbeknown to the celebrity who paid him and went on his jolly way, the Seeker was left trembling and shattered by what he had seen and heard, and the act he had committed. That day he had vowed never again to kill a healthy animal. This even included fish (and this made it difficult to continue as an ordinary veterinarian). That day had shown him that money, the obedience to Mammon, could be the source of the utmost evil.

Now he stood there steadfastly, looking directly at the demonic structures before him. Then something happened. The 'arms' of the demons started to shiver, to convulse, to spiral, and the surrounding blackness started to become lighter. It was as if a faint light had been lit deep within their structures. The light became stronger and stronger, and after a while a rift appeared in the area where the chest or heart should have been, although it is impossible to talk about such things in the form that the demons had now assumed.

Then a sound like breaking glass was heard and, before his very eyes, the demons simply disappeared.

All was over. He stayed for a while. Then he went home.

Chapter 12

Rebuilding the Altar in the Cosmos. The Three Layers.
The Karmic Consequences for Present-day Culture

After the Seeker had transformed the three demons, he finally came to understand more of the past actions that had bound him to the demons in the first place.

He had used his powers, in connection with the strength of the demons, to suppress others. He had used his fellow human beings to gain power in both the astral world, concerning the feeling body, and the etheric world, in the realm of the life forces; in the elemental world, by using demons and demonic powers to fulfil his wishes, and finally in the physical realm, by forcing people to stay connected to a particular mystery centre of ancient Atlantis. This was a threefold (or fourfold) sin.

Many of his fellow high priests and keepers of the mysteries had also done what he had done, and because of this they had avoided incarnating on Earth ever since – although some of them had dared to incarnate in times of war, for example during and before both World Wars.

*

I will now describe in greater detail the Atlantean pyramid and its central section or room, as the Seeker described it to me. This central part was the command room or the control centre, if you will. From this room huge amounts of energy – etheric energy – could be harnessed, gathered or stored, and used for good or evil. This etheric energy was gathered from many sources: from nature, from trees, from animals, from the strange thought-forms created by the magicians at that time, and from the human beings making up the group, the clan or congregation living around the great pyramid. All this energy was stored or condensed, so to speak, in the room of mirrors and crystals. All were forbidden to enter this room apart from the high priest, the oracle and their closest co-workers. The etheric energy was stored in such a way that it could be used only by the leaders or directors of the pyramid.

The initial intention with this etheric energy was to use it for good – this was the intention of the gods. But man´s greed for power is creative, and through the centuries the leading groups had managed to deviate from the divine law, and thus made it possible to use this energy for egoistic purposes. The effect of the energy then became quite different from what was intended; it became destructive. This is also the case today: etheric energy can only be used for good, for moral purposes, otherwise – if, through deviations from the light path, it is used egoistically – it becomes dangerous. The effect of this energy is also enormous. The etheric energy harvested from even one person was enough to keep the whole activity of the society, and the pyramid, going.

In the beginning, this energy was used for good, but then – under the influence of the dark powers, the adversaries – the use slowly turned to serve the self, the egoistical purposes of the leading group of the area that was located in the pyramid. This malign use eventually caused the destruction of the whole Atlantean continent.

A particular occult group working in Germany today, with the mystery intention of making etheric energy available for common use, considers that the etheric energy coming from a single human would be sufficient to power the entire city of New York, for example. Thus, we can understand that etheric energy is of enormous power.

Today it is of crucial importance that we again become able to use this etheric energy for the good of all humanity, and thus free ourselves from the use of electrical energy, which is destroying our environment and our climate and is very ahrimanic and pathological in its functions.

This etheric energy can of course also be used in a darker way, in the way of black magic, serving the sole interest of egoistic individuals. Today this should not be allowed to happen! That is how Atlantis was finally destroyed.

The Seeker had twice seen this ancient knowledge being used in an egotistical way in the contemporary world, and I am able to recognize this too. These two places are in Italy and India. The most obvious manifestation of this technology is visible in the Italian group, where they even call the room where the etheric energy is harnessed, 'the Selfic Chamber'. In this room is focused the energy allegedly stolen from many individuals – even etheric energy taken from trees. In this so-called Selfic Chamber, this energy, this etheric force, is used according to the personal wishes of the group's leader – who has now passed away, although another leader has surely taken his place and may even be acting as a channel for the original leader.

As I have said, 15,000 years ago such egoistic use of etheric forces led to the destruction of a whole continent.

Much time was spent in the Seeker's Selfic Chamber within that Atlantean pyramid, situated in what today is known as Ireland. In this chamber, the energy of his congregation – the followers, or let us say obedient 'slaves' – were gathered. This energy was used, among other things, to bind the followers even more tightly than through the use of a magic tie around one's neck. In this connection, it was important to hinder the free flow of energy between the centres of thinking, feeling and the will, located respectively in the northern, central and southern parts of Ireland – and also located in the head, the chest and the abdomen of individual human beings.

The Atlantean chamber was formed like a cupola with a small door at the bottom and a hole at the top. In this hole was placed a huge crystal that could direct and also make use of the etheric energy. The walls of the chamber were constructed of multiple layers of glass, gold-sheet, mirrors and small crystals. It worked like a hybrid of a condenser and a laser. In this room they could gather, store and direct the etheric energy and use it according to their wishes and intentions. As it was etheric, it could be used for growth, but also for death and destruction. It had many other purposes too, such as construction of new species (as with today's genetic manipulations) and procreation, and research into the past. Numerous other entities were there, created to be used as slaves, to work in the fields and forests and for personal pleasure.

This was the Seeker's and his closest followers' holy room, and they all gathered there in the time of destruction for safety. In their self-aggrandizement and arrogance, they thought they would be protected. The Seeker still remembers the destruction of this chamber, as well as of the whole pyramid. (The destruction of Atlantis actually went on for hundreds of years and three phases. The final area to be destroyed was the north-eastern region, where the three 'Irish' mystery places were situated.) Below is his recollection.

*

One day the whole earth trembled then erupted, and the masses of water flowed over us like a tsunami.

My dearest love was taken by the deluge as it broke through and crushed 'the room of crystals and mirrors'. She fell slowly backwards in a chaos of water, whirling crystals and broken mirrors. She was paralyzed by fear, stretching out her right hand towards me, crying for help and salvation, looking directly into my eyes. I stretched out my right hand too, but did not reach her. I desperately tried to rescue her, stretching my arm out further, but the water took her away.

She drowned, but that was not the end.

I was taken by the water. In a strange mood of altruism, quite alien for me at that time, I managed to save one of my slaves, one of my egoistic inventions based on black magic – a creature of mixed human and animal form.

That brought about a final realization in my condemned soul, which later, in the emerging new epoch, would help me be redeemed.

Then I drowned, but that was not the end.

*

Our friend the Seeker had later dared to incarnate, due to one single small event that happened during the 'third destruction'. This event had given him the courage to continue his development with the rest of the human race. It might seem to have been an insignificant event, but it had far reaching consequences.

Due to the immense misuse of etheric and physical powers, the Atlantean initiates had created thought forms of strange creatures like the cyclops and giants, and these creatures had been forced to work for the initiated rulers. The rulers had no compassion for these life-forms and used them as they pleased. They knew that such actions would create an enormously heavy karma, but with the powers they possessed, the paying back of this karma would not be difficult. Little did they know that the abilities and powers that they needed to restore this karma would be lost when the Atlantean period ended.

In the moment when the masses of water poured over the remains of the old Atlantean continent, our friend the Seeker had come across one of these creatures struggling to save its own life. It was a mixture of a lion and a bull, and it was fighting the rising waters. For one moment the Seeker felt pity on this wretched creature and used the powers he had that were still intact to separate the bull and the lion so that it could save itself. (As mentioned, the Atlanteans lost their ability to manipulate the etheric realm during this cataclysmic disaster, and were later unable to rectify what they had done wrong.) This action implanted a seed of compassion in the Seeker, that corrupt old Atlantean initiate, so that he could see a possibility to incarnate in the new world that arose after the destruction.

But the demons attached to these former actions and to his misuse of power were – as we have seen – intact, as were the karmic results of his sins. To repent and redeem these three levels of misdeeds in our time, he had to restore what he had destroyed.

Now that he was free from the demons, he was also able to restore his karma. He was free to rebuild his old altar in the cosmos in its threefold power – in thinking, in feeling and in will – in the astral, etheric and even in its physical form. He also understood the karmic consequences relating to today's society.

The first destruction was brought about by sin on the level of the astral – greed and power.

The second destruction was brought about by sin on the level of the etheric – by the misuse of powers of life and growth for the benefit of oneself.

The third and final destruction was brought about by the misuse of the physical powers – by the misuse of the Earth itself.

Today we can see the same pattern repeated.

Humanity started with sin on the astral level – sinning within our feelings, our lust and our greed.

Then we continued to sin in the etheric realm. Today we are in the midst of such misuse of these etheric forces. Through genetic manipulation, through life-destroying poisons and through bringing death to life, we are actually in the second destruction.

When we start to manipulate matter itself, creating new substances and using physical powers for our own intentions, we will and must face the third destruction. We already have started with this.

To counteract the above, the Seeker had to build a new altar in the cosmos – an altar created from all three layers – through which healing may occur. This altar is a human altar, consisting of a circle or group of people that are gathered to create and receive healing for the world, through the central power of the Christ. The activation of the Christ force in each member of this circle will open a portal between the astral world, the etheric world and the physical world, and will celebrate the healing of the world and humanity. This will bring a sacramental offering in space and time. From this altar, a force will go out that will influence the whole of the Earth and the whole of mankind.

First, the circling etheric energy will rise towards the sky, bringing down the healing force of thinking through *cosmic humour*, down through all nine hierarchies – plus the three realms of the Father-Trinity – of the celestial realms.

Then the healing force of Christ will penetrate through the will of the depths of the Earth itself and bring healing up through all nine layers of the Earth, plus the three realms of the Mother-Trinity.

Then, in the last phase, the healing force of Christ will spread out towards the surrounding world and bring the healing force back through all fourteen layers of the wide expanses of the world.

Then the communion is complete, and the altar will have served its purpose in the redemption of the sins of old.*

---

*The full description of this method and of the 3-4-7-9-12 layers of reality is described and further explained in my book *Spiritual Medicine*, especially in the third part.

Chapter 13

The Way into the Future. The Transformation of Evil

The knowledge and experiences that the Seeker gained when facing and transforming the three demons, made him engage in the question of how to bring the three powers of the cosmos into today's society – into the consciousness of his fellow human beings – to enable the great possibilities of thinking, feeling and will into the future. This should have been his task during the Atlantean period, but he failed and instead used the three powers for his own benefit. Now he could start again on his real work.

He had to make his fellow human beings aware of the three forces in the cosmos, and to what extent they are violated every day.

In *thinking* it is easy to understand how we may sin or make mistakes. We know that some thoughts are wrong and that some are right. That 2 + 2 = 4 will always be so, and not 5.

In *feeling* it is also easy to understand what is right and what is wrong. We experience how negative feelings create negativity in the world and destroy us. Yet many people do not see or understand how nationalism and chauvinism, experienced for example through football, is a sin in the astral realm of existence. Or how the joy experienced through hunting or shooting an animal, or fishing, is likewise a sin. Even how every single lie is like an explosion in the spiritual world.

In *will* it is even harder to understand how we sin. The will, the most powerful force in the cosmos, is very poorly understood by human beings. The power of will is in all actions, in all movements, in all work that we perform. When we dig a hole, when we write a letter, when we kiss someone – all this includes will, cosmic will. And all actions that are *not* done out of love are a sin to the universe. This is difficult to fathom. But we have to fathom and understand this in order to be able to move into the future.

We have to understand that we are the vessels through which these cosmic forces or powers can enter earthly development, and that this development is of the utmost importance today.

'Is there any hope for this civilisation?', the Seeker once asked me.

My own thoughts and response to him were as follows:

Of utmost importance

Today the knowledge and insight of the spiritual world is vanishing rapidly, as materialism takes its hold. Fewer and fewer people believe in God.

Respect for other life forms, trees and animals, as well as for non-material beings, has lessened, and egoistic materialism is progressing.

Culture is trembling under the weight of ignorance, and from where I stand I cannot see any rescue or salvation.

Our culture will vanish as all other cultures have vanished, and the cause of our destruction will be ever-progressing materialism and egoism that will eventually culminate in a War of All Against All.

The knowledge presented in this book, along with all other similar knowledge, will be carried over to the next culture by a small number of people who have grasped the need for spirituality, and together they will create a new culture of spiritual and brotherly love.

Closing Remarks to Part II

So, what happened with the demons in the end?

During the long period of their existence, they had become quite powerful. But now they were transformed at all levels and spheres of their existence; in the astral, the etheric and the physical realms – relating to feeling, thinking and the will. They could now participate in the development of Earth as light-filled elementals.

Evil changing into good is very powerful, as illustrated in the Bible story, *The Parable of the Lost Son:*

> Jesus continued: 'There was a man who had two sons. The younger one said to his father, "Father, give me my share of the estate." So he divided his property between them.
>
> Not long after that, the younger son got together all he had, set off for a distant country and there squandered his wealth in wild living. After he had spent everything, there was a severe famine in that whole country, and he began to be in need. So he went and hired himself out to a citizen of that country, who sent him to his fields to feed pigs. He longed to fill his stomach with the pods that the pigs were eating, but no one gave him anything.
>
> When he came to his senses, he said, "How many of my father's hired servants have food to spare, and here I am starving to death! I will set out and go back to my father and say to him: Father, I have sinned against heaven and against you. I am no longer worthy to be called your son; make me like one of your hired servants." So he got up and went to his father.
>
> But while he was still a long way off, his father saw him and was filled with compassion for him; he ran to his son, threw his arms around him and kissed him.
>
> The son said to him, "Father, I have sinned against heaven and against you. I am no longer worthy to be called your son."
>
> But the father said to his servants, "Quick! Bring the best robe and put it on him. Put a ring on his finger and sandals on his feet. Bring the fattened calf and kill it. Let's have a

feast and celebrate. For this son of mine was dead and is
alive again; he was lost and is found." So they began to celebrate.

Meanwhile, the older son was in the field. When he came
near the house, he heard music and dancing. So he called
one of the servants and asked him what was going on.
"Your brother has come," he replied, "and your father has
killed the fattened calf because he has him back safe and
sound."

The older brother became angry and refused to go in. So
his father went out and pleaded with him. But he answered
his father, "Look! All these years I've been slaving for you
and never disobeyed your orders. Yet you never gave me
even a young goat so I could celebrate with my friends. But
when this son of yours who has squandered your property
with prostitutes comes home, you kill the fattened calf for
him!"

"My son," the father said, "you are always with me, and
everything I have is yours. But we had to celebrate and be
glad, because this brother of yours was dead and is alive
again; he was lost and is found."''*

This book tells a true story. Although this truth can't be proved, it is
true for our friend the Seeker. Such truths can only be experienced in
the spiritual world, in a subjective/objective reality.

Although this story stretches out in time over 22 years and continues to unravel, the first part was written during a period of two
weeks in the autumn of 2015, and the second part over two weeks
in the autumn of 2017. When one first starts to write about these
things in an attempt to make such events public to the consciousness of the world, 'something' starts to help, as if spiritual forces
want to expose such realities. One starts to remember more and
more details. During one's sleep, pictures and places become imaginations of the soul. An inner voice begins to speak; sleep becomes
lighter as if one were almost awake, enabling additional aspects of
the complex process of opening old karma and old wisdom.

I watched as my friend opened his soul to me, revealing his karma,
paying back consciously, accepting his past actions and delving into

*Luke 15:11-32.

the deep, deep and far-off past. I watched him every day in this process, and noticed several changes in his behaviour, changes in the way he saw himself.

The Seeker told me about the deep and unexpected changes in his soul that left him wondering if he was actually still himself; if his legs were indeed his own. To use the Seeker's own words:

> When waking up in the morning, I often spend a long time remembering who I am, finding out which incarnation I am presently in... Time has become so fluctuating and transparent that I feel as if I no longer live in the twenty-first century.

I observed him many times sitting on his veranda or walking in his garden. He felt the presence of the birds and the flowers in a different way than before, as if his relationship to them had changed, from 'owning' them to becoming 'part' of them, to loving them. It was as if his love of the world had changed; it had become selfless – without wanting anything back from it.

What changes in your mind, in your soul, in your spirit, when a 25,000-year-old karma is paid off; when, perhaps, a 40,000-year-old debt is settled, is repaid, is straightened out? When you have realized the power of the Christ? When you have seen your demons change into light? What changes?

With such huge questions, what can one say? What can one answer to questions like that?

Something changes, that is for sure. The Seeker tried to explain it to me. The closest he came was as follows:

> The light you perceive changes into selflessness.
>   The love you feel humbles. Yes, the love you feel growing within your heart becomes free; free from wanting, free from attachment, free from cravings, free from desire, free from hunger, sexuality, thirst...

My friend stuttered as he searched for words, for he was at a loss in explaining what had happened within him. *But I saw the light in his eyes.*

I would come across him as he read the Bible, weeping. He did not know why, but the love he found there, in the descriptions of Christ Jesus, touched him so deeply that his tears streamed freely.

It seems that exploring past karma and past incarnations has a freeing effect on the soul, releasing something that has been bound in the past for eons; especially when one has had such a dark and violent past as the Seeker had.

Now, as I try to bring the second part of this book to a close, additional memories push their way into the open. It is as if I become one – or something makes me one – with a portal from past worlds, from the spiritual backgrounds of our existence.

I don't want to stop writing, although I know I must. Every book has its frame, and I cannot just keep on writing... But if more is to be written, it should contain additional information about the story of the Seeker during the third and last destruction of Atlantis... Why did the Seeker dare to reincarnate, in opposition to his friends, the *non-incarnated Atlanteans*, and what could be learned from that experience relating to our own time and civilization?

May this story give inspiration to those who wish to explore past times, past lives, past karma and, in the light of the old wisdom, gaze forward towards the future.

PART III

Introduction to Part III

The Astral, Etheric and Physical Worlds in Relation to Initiation, Demonic Activity and Karma

I did not see or meet my friend the Seeker for eight months, but when I did meet him again, he had much to tell me. He was sitting in a downtown café, drinking his favourite cappuccino. I sat opposite him, and for some time we just looked at each other. After quite a long pause, he opened his mouth and said: 'Do you remember the story from the *Edda*, the story about the three "Nornes"?'*

I looked at him in amazement. He continued:

> You know, there were three Norns, three women presenting the karma to the newborn child, according to Nordic knowledge. And according to the Northern way of initiation, one always meets karma in three ways and on all three levels: in the astral, in the etheric and in the physical realm. Thus, all in all, in nine ways. Hercules had to perform nine deeds that were karmic, but as he cheated somewhat, or rather received unexpected help with three of the deeds, he had to perform three extra ones – a total of twelve deeds. Well, we all have to perform these nine levels or deeds in order to restore our karma.

He paused for a while, then went on:

> I guess the fact that Hercules cheated implies that karma is active or has to be dealt with in three additional ways at an even higher level – maybe the upper spiritual level. So, in reality there should be *four* Nornes. As time and space are illusory, all that takes place also takes place in both the future and the past; in the physical, etheric, astral and spiritual realms simultaneously. That is the secret behind synchronicity.

---

*The Norns in Norse mythology are 'female' entities who are said to rule the destiny of gods and human beings. They roughly correspond to other controllers of human destiny elsewhere in European mythology, such as the Fates.

My friend sighed, then continued:

> Reality is so complicated, and it becomes more and more
> clear to me that the physical part of this reality might be the
> most difficult to understand. This physical reality is, during
> the evolution of our material cosmos, impregnated with
> matter, which further disturbs our vision and understand-
> ing of the physical world. Most people think that the terms
> physical and material are equivalent expressions, but that is
> the grand illusion. This misunderstanding also gives rise to
> the misinterpretation of time as linear. Time as a linear func-
> tion is totally due to the illusion of material substance being
> equal to physical existence.
>
> You know, I really thought that I had conquered all my
> demons, but I was wrong. I had met and overcome those that
> existed in the astral and the etheric realms of existence, but
> little did I know that, by working with demons for such a long
> time, they imprinted their structures deep in my body, deep in
> my very soul, deep in the physical body and simultaneously
> in the spiritual realm. This challenge is now my task, my duty,
> and it is with this huge problem that I am now working.

I had to ponder this long and hard. So, after having conquered his
demons in the astral realm, believing that was all (as told in Part I of
this book), and in the etheric realm, also believing that this was all (in
Part II), the Seeker now had to conquer the demonic forces within himself, in the physical realm of his own body and in the material/physical
reality itself.

The laws of these three realms are completely different, just as the
three Norns are completely different. Their names (*Ve*, *Vilje* and *Ver-
dande*) are as different as the past, the present and the future – which
is actually their meaning – even though time is an illusion and only
relevant in the material realm.

To understand the above, we have to acquire a somewhat deeper
insight into the mysteries of:

- *The physical realm*, which is totally different from the etheric, elemental – even all three realms of the elemental world – and astral realms.
  However, it is no less spiritual, but actually more so. The physical realm
  is often confused with the material realm, but – as already mentioned –
  they are totally different.

- *Karma*, which works totally differently in the astral realm, the etheric realm, the elemental world and the physical realm.
- *The Doppelgänger*, who works and also appears also quite differently in the different realms.
- *The Guardian of the Threshold*, who gives his warnings and advice very differently in the three realms.
- *The Southern and the Northern streams of initiation*. Both ways can be used to access the two higher realms.

Some of these aspects have already been expanded upon, whilst some will be explained in this final part of our book.

Chapter 14

The Seeker's Deceit

The Seeker continued his monologue as we sat in that café:

> I have now found that the imprint of my past deeds are also in my physical body. This is so strange for me, as I had never thought that karma is *threefold* – even *ninefold* or *twelvefold*, for that matter. We all talk about karma as if it is a single thing, not understanding its complexity. And now I am confronted with one more aspect of my 40,000-year-old karma.
>
> This old karma was about misusing the energy of other human beings, or even the thought-forms of old Atlantis. I had the power and ability to interfere with the streams of the body, the connections between thinking, feeling and will, conscious and unconscious thought-power – and I used this energy for my own power and actions.
>
> I stopped this misuse a long time ago, and for this I – or rather, my daughter – got back parts of my healing ability. Nevertheless, in a certain part of my actions and work I still misused others´ energy, and discovering this has been a crucial part of resolving karma in the physical realm. I actually did not know about this misuse, and to discover it was rather a shock for me.

So, how did this misuse take place? The Seeker looked at me directly and intensively, and started to explain:

> You know how for years I have been lecturing all over Europe and America, and how I loved doing this work. And why did I like lecturing? It has to do with both the contents of my lectures but even more so with the groups of people listening. My listeners are, for the most part, at least 95% younger women who are spiritually-inclined. When I lecture or teach such groups in spiritual matters, I receive immense quantities of energy from these women listening – an incredible energy that makes me feel strong, invincible and 'kingly'.
>
> This energy should be described in further detail. It is different from the energy of the cosmos, which can be received

both directly and indirectly. The 'direct' way is straight from the planets, the zodiac or from the wide expanses of the cosmos behind the zodiac. The indirect way is when this energy penetrates the Earth and is then mirrored back into the body. The first kind works spiritually in an up-building fashion, whilst the second way works ahrimanically, in a destructive way. Still, both streams feel strong and powerful, and feel beneficial to the receiver if they don't realize the difference.

We can see the same concerning the energy received from nature, which can also be received both directly and indirectly. The direct stream is spiritual and the indirect form, which passes through the Earth before entering the human body, is ahrimanic. We can also receive energy from animals, again in two ways; directly or via the dark forces of the Earth. The direct stream of energy from animals, at least the higher animals – I will not elaborate now on the lower forms or insects – communicates with human energy through the group-souls of the various animals. This exchange happens in the upper layers of the atmosphere, in the so called 'Thermosphere', 90 kilometres above the Earth, where the Northern Lights express themselves. From there, it can enter humans directly or indirectly, as already described. The Sami children are taught to be afraid of the animal energy coming from or through the Northern Lights, as they can become 'crazy' when animal energy enters them, both directly or indirectly. They are told to hide in the snow when the Northern Lights come too close.

But now back to the energy coming from female groups listening to spiritual lectures... The energy received from a group of women can enter my energetic body in two ways (though it is of the same kind, in my experience it is like two different types, just like the energy received from the cosmos, nature or animals). One stream comes through the upper part, the head or the sense organs, and then streams down into the body and through all the organs, building them up in a good, 'up-building' way. This stream follows the blood vessels, thus connecting it to the cosmic Christ-force, as Christ is connected to the blood. This stream resembles the already-described direct streams, from cosmos or nature.

The other stream goes through the sense-organs and then directly to the lower part of the body, to the area of the sexual organs – down even into the Earth – and from there streams up through all the nerves. This makes it ahrimanic, as ahrimanic forces dominate the nerves. This stream is negative, full of power and can be used to perform all kinds of darker magic. I used this kind of energy in ancient Atlantis, thousands of years ago, and this energy made me capable of performing all my dark deeds.

So, what is the cause of the difference between these two streams? The first stream is imbued with the understanding, with the 'I'-conscious power of the listeners, and this energy gives rise to good deeds, to constructive 'up-building' of the body and the relationship between the lecturer and the listener.

The other stream is darker for two reasons: either that the listeners have not understood what is said with their conscious minds, or that they have 'impure' feelings for the lecturer. This last kind of energy works in a very immoral and seductive way. It is exactly what I sought for and used in my darker work when I craved power as an oracle in ancient Atlantis – an energy that could be used for black magic and which eventually brought about the destruction of the whole continent.

During my many years of lecturing, this form of energy became more and more dominant without me becoming aware of this development. I somehow got entangled in the net of this ahrimanic energy, which in time also became imbued with luciferic energy.

The interesting aspect was that I was starting to understand this kind of energy; I was on the threshold of 'seeing' it and thus becoming able to free myself from it. But then the dark forces intervened.

One day, one of the female listeners came to me after a lecture and said she wanted to be my lover. She said that she loved me, and had loved me for many lifetimes. And, as I was then still at the beginning of understanding this darker form of energy and had not yet realized that it would lead to destruction, I wanted to make this stream of energy much stronger and so I succumbed. I failed my family, my wife, my destiny, my friends and my children and stayed in a relationship with this woman, as lovers, for three years (note, *three* again). And, to make it all even more hopeless, shortly after this relationship started I engaged in yet another relationship, as if I could not get enough.

The old misuse of dark and sexual energy had again started. And I was entangled in this net for three years. Three full years!

I knew that I had to get out, and I did indeed manage to get out of one of the relationships (the second one), but the other gave so much energy that I did not get out – at least not voluntarily.

Even though I chose to stay in these relationships for three years, I was fully aware that I was doing wrong; that I was lying and deceiving my loving wife, and this caused me a lot of regret, pain and mental imbalance. But still I carried on with it. It is almost impossible for me to believe this now.

To be able really to understand how destructive such vampirism is, the Seeker had to experience the full and whole implications of pain and destruction of his actions. My friend continued:

So, once I had understood the situation, karma made it even worse – but then also as a salvation for me. Divine forces interfered and engaged, and my beloved wife found out. The deceit was revealed. This helped me to get out of these destructive connections.

Of course, she was hurt, angry and devastated. We were both hurt and devastated, but the love we had, and have, for each other saved us.

But before our love made it possible to repair the relationship, everything fell apart. My whole life was shattered. The previous relationship I had with my wife that was good, now crumbled at its roots. My children realized what a liar I was, my patients doubted me – even doubted my ability to heal them. How can an infidel heal others?

This was a terrible time, as I fully understood that the 'energy-game' I had been playing really was a destructive and ahrimanic power-play involving many innocent people.

Here, the Seeker took a long and deep breath, and looked at me strangely. It was a look that expressed regret, insight and pain. I was personally shocked, as the friend I knew was a highly spiritual person, and I had not expected this. I knew of his work with karma, but I had certainly not expected this!

I understood, now, that I had to add a third part to my book on the Seeker's former misuse of dark powers. This new part also had to contain an explanation of the multiplicity of karma and how to work with it in the physical/material realm.

'So, how are you working today to transform this karma – this karma imbued in your physical body?', I asked finally, after a long silence. The Seeker gazed at me for a long time.

'I am in the very middle of this work just now', he said.

> When I understood that my old karma was still in my physical body, I started to search for the area or place where it could be found. You see, everything that is imbued or created in the physical body is also to be found there. I am not speaking now of the material body – this body is just an illusion, a part of the physical body impregnated with material substance which we call molecules or atoms. The 'real' physical body is vast and far-reaching, and when we die we see truly how big our physical body is. It is as vast as the cosmos itself, containing much more than we can ever imagine. In this physical body I started to search for the area where the lower stream or streams of energy gathered and became 'active' – where they became used or made themselves available for the adversarial forces, the ahrimanic and luciferic forces.
>
> I have long experience in searching within myself (and others) for 'disruptions', hidden trauma, hidden 'rooms' or demonic forces – or even demons in the physical body. This was one of the primary abilities I developed in my life. As early as the age of 10, I could 'scan' physical bodies and find pathological areas like foreign bodies, scars or demonic and dark entities.[*]
>
> I searched my body – my physical but not material body (otherwise what I found would have shown on an x-ray) – and

---

[*]This is explained and further described in *Experiences from the Threshold* (op. cit.).

discovered a dark chamber that I had not seen previously. The chamber was cubic, situated directly under the heart, between it and the diaphragm. It had three doors, one leading up, one downwards and one to the right side.

Similar rooms, with three entrances or exits, have been known to me for a long time. This structure is usually used by the dark forces, the adversaries, to 'tap' energy from their victims. Black magicians of all ages have known this secret, that enables them to harvest energy. It is often used without the victim's knowledge. And now, unbelievably, I had one within myself!

The Seeker went on to describe the 'room', that he had found and entered, in the following way:

It was without windows or any other form of light. It smelled rotten and the grass growing there was half dead, yellow-green, bent and suffering. There was some kind of light in the room, but it was impossible to see where this light came from. Through the lower entrance, many kinds of energies could enter – energies that come from the Earth, or at least energies that have gone through the earthly realm. From this direction also came the sexualized energies and those that have not been worked-through consciously – for example, those that entered during or after I gave spiritual lectures to a mainly female audience.

Through the middle door or exit, the energy from this hidden room could be harvested by demonic forces. The upper door, however, was firmly shut, clogged with dust and dirt from centuries of being closed.

The Seeker continued with his explanations:

The middle exit or entrance was very interesting to study. Through this door the dark forces had access and could tap the sort of energy they needed to perform their dark deeds. This door also communicated with the heart, and this opening had a strange one- and two-way communication. Through this doorway, the dark forces could hinder the 'real' spirituality entering the heart, and at the same time feed vampirically on the heart energy or spirituality of the human being. Through this opening, the adversarial forces could hinder Christ from entering the heart.

I was shocked when finding this hidden room or chamber. I had no knowledge or conscious experience of it. I watched it for days and weeks, not knowing what to do. Then I started to build a window in the right wall of the room, the side of the luciferic forces, just beside the middle doorway. Light began to stream in, sunlight, Christ Sun, enlightening my head, warming my heart, so that good might come of the work I had now started. And, day by day, a change could be traced, and was to be observed.

When my wife told all our family and friends about my deceit, I was at first quite devastated by shame, but then I started to see the benefits of telling people about my betrayal. It is like in the old fairy tales, when the troll is killed or turned to stone as the light shines on it.

Collective consciousness is a strange thing.

The Seeker repeated the last sentence, gazing into the distance.

It has a power of its own. And this power relates to the light, the Light of the Christ that can shine into the darkness, just as it is stated in the opening words of the Gospel of St John. But the real strength of this is only 'when two or three are gathered together in my name...'

In this way, the light that shone through the newly made window was made accessible to the rest of my friends and family, and as such gained a universal importance.

Chapter 15

A Family Karma. The Universal Importance of the Seeker's Repentance and Light Work

As we continued to sit in that café, the Seeker elaborated on his descriptions of the 'chamber' he had discovered within himself:

> Day by day that dark room changed, becoming lighter and lighter, the grass growing greener and stronger, the air becoming fresher and more fragrant. The room was larger than I had thought at first glance. One day I made a discovery of huge implications. I found a wooden building in one of the corners, an old building with a timber frame. There was light in the windows and a fire on the stove. I knocked at the door and it was opened by a diseased member of my family, Gunnar. He greeted me warmly, as if he was expecting me, and gave me a friendly kiss. He seemed to understand that I was not yet dead, but still let me in. I entered the house and to my amazement discovered that the entire abode was inhabited by diseased members of my family; members that had already passed the threshold and into the realm of death. They all lived in this cosy and warm house. But, on closer observation, almost everyone I saw there was male – there were virtually no women in this wooden house! I was bewildered.
>
> I recalled that almost all members of my family had refrained from becoming influenced by Christianity, staying in the old blood-relationships of family and tribe. So, instead of going further in the spiritual world after death, they had remained in this cosy house. In old times, when the family bonds were strong, almost all families had such houses in the spiritual world.
>
> But why was this house built in a corner of the dark room that I had discovered? Was this room part of the family karma? Were the forces that sought for female sexuality, or one might say the forces of unconscious spirituality, a family weakness. Was this *family karma*?

After finding this room I contacted several male members of my family to ask how the old male members of my family had related to women. Their answers confirmed my suspicions. Almost all male members – I did not ask the female members – were more or less dependent or addicted to these forces, all indulging in infidelity. In this way, they were all bound to this stream, and thus bound in this dark room – although having been able to build a cosy family home, almost like a private Valhalla.* Maybe such houses were the origin of the stories of Valhalla?

---

*In Norse mythology, Valhalla is a majestic hall located in Asgard, ruled over by the god Odin. Chosen by Odin, half of those who die in combat travel to Valhalla upon death.

Conclusion

From what we have seen, karma is multidimensional, a living matrix, existing in several realms and relating to several different entities.

Our deeds are inscribed in all dimensions and realms of the cosmos, and – as time and space are illusions – our deeds will have an impact in all times: in the past and in the future.

Our work to restore karma and the restoration of our own 'dark rooms' or 'chambers' will also have importance for our friends and family, as we are eternally bound and connected to bonds of both blood and spirit, as well as karmic bonds.

Our work with karma, which is related to the whole Earth, as well as to the Lord of this Earth, the Christ, will as such have an immense importance for the entire cosmos and its eternal meaning.

And as for the demons... Can anything more be said of them, now that they were defeated and transformed – even in the physical realm of existence?

My old friend the Seeker tried to make a summary for me. It seems apposite to end with these words:

> It was the only way for me to be free of my old karma: first to go through resolution in the astral world, then in the etheric and elemental worlds and then, finally, to experience the results of such karma in the physical/material world.
>
> Karma – that is inscribed in the Earth just as Christ inscribed the ill deeds of the woman accused of adultery in the Earth with his finger – has to be resolved through forgiveness in the physical world. From this description of Christ's actions in the Bible, it would appear that the physical deed of adultery and its heavy consequences are archetypical as the final stage of karmic resolution.
>
> And the forgiveness that the Seeker received from his wife marked the final end of his 40,000-year-old karma.

Books to challenge  *your perception of reality*

A message from Clairview

We are an independent publishing company with a focus on cutting-edge, non-fiction books. Our innovative list covers current affairs and politics, health, the arts, history, science and spirituality. But regardless of subject, our books have a common link: they all question conventional thinking, dogmas and received wisdom.

Despite being a small company, our list features some big names, such as Booker Prize winner Ben Okri, literary giant Gore Vidal, world leader Mikhail Gorbachev, modern artist Joseph Beuys and natural childbirth pioneer Michel Odent.

So, check out our full catalogue online at
www.clairviewbooks.com
and join our emailing list for news on new titles.

office@clairviewbooks.com

CLAIRVIEW